THE RHYTHM
OF RUNNING

Jim Hunt

ISBN: 978-1-60679-431-9
Library of Congress Control Number: 2018941744
Book layout: Cheery Sugabo
Cover design: Cheery Sugabo
Front cover photo: © Jiro Mochizuki/Image of Sports/Newscom via ZUMA Press

Coaches Choice
P.O. Box 1828
Monterey, CA 93942
www.coacheschoice.com

ACKNOWLEDGMENTS

Many thanks to my wife and family for their complete support, which made it possible to spend the time that I needed to develop my coaching skills.

A special thanks to Jo Ann, my wife, Tracy Gale, my daughter, and Megan and Sarra Gale, my granddaughters, for the hours they spent deciphering and typing my terrible penmanship.

CONTENTS

PREFACE

With the hundreds of books and thousands of articles already written on the subject of training to race in endurance events, why would I want to write a book on the subject? I believe there are some misguided concepts of training to race in endurance events that most coaches adhere to, but which I propose can be changed. First, that you must establish an aerobic base through running slow-to-moderate paced mileage before you can begin developing other physiological variables that are involved in training. Second, that running endurance events is not considered a "skill" event. Third, that endurance running is not a "speed"-oriented event. Fourth, that training and racing endurance events do not require dynamic movements.

This book provides guidelines that will apply to all levels of runners including youth, high school, collegiate, and elite post-collegiate, as well as recreation and master competitors who want to improve their running and racing ability from the 800 meters to the marathon. It will cover all aspects on what a person needs to do to reach their optimal genetic level of ability in competition. In particular, it will include a much-neglected phase of training, the neuromuscular aspects of running.

The title of my book is *The Rhythm of Running*, and the goals I have set forth to accomplish with my training scheme are as follows:
- Gold medal running form development
- Speed enhancement
- Functional muscle strength improvement
- Better lactate conversion
- Overall endurance development

INTRODUCTION

Over the past four decades, American coaches have basically been training their runners on high-mileage tempo runs, fast intervals, and overall hard work efforts as the answer to running fast race times in endurance events. Most coaches and runners ignore the fact that foot strike time, turnover rate, and running economy have a significant bearing on racing ability. I think this point is exemplified by a conversation I had with Ed Eyestone, two-time USA Olympic Marathon qualifier, at the 1988 U.S. Olympic Marathon Trials. We discussed both his propensity to overstride and his excessive vertical lift while racing. Although Ed acknowledged it was a problem, he preferred to work on his strengths, rather than spend training time trying to correct his weaknesses.

Another example I noted was that of Bob Kennedy, former American record holder in the 3k and 5k meters. I counted his stride rate at 192 per minute, while he was running earlier in the race. When he increased to a faster running velocity, he did it by lengthening his stride, while maintaining the same turnover rate. If Kennedy had also increased his stride rate to 196 per minute and used an ankle-over-knee heel cycle, like many of the East Africans do, he may have been able to run 10 seconds faster in a typical 5k race. The point being that an endurance athlete's running rhythm, the best combination of stride rate and stride length, determines the speed with which the runner can run a race.

Why can't American coaches teach their young aspiring endurance runners how to run fast? The answer is they can. It is as simple as teaching the runners proper running mechanics and developing functional muscle strength beginning the first day of practice and continuing to do so throughout the entire season. Coaches can identify and correct poor running posture, and slow foot and arm action, as well as change strained running habits to running relaxed without wasting energy. This objective should be accomplished concurrently, while jump-starting the runner's $\dot{V}O_2max$ development.

If you, as a runner or as a coach, want to work on all aspects of running conditioning and become a complete runner, consider using the training schemes outlined in this book. Athletes of all abilities can follow my same basic training scheme to develop their potential level of fitness. It is just a matter of making adjustments within the training scheme to fit the fitness level of each athlete.

CHAPTER 1 ━━━━━━━━━━━
The Need to Run

Movement is synonymous with life! We, as animals, move primarily on our own power by harnessing chemical energy found in our muscular system. Throughout the millions of past years of animal evolution, there has been selective pressure in some species to be able to travel faster, farther, and do it more economically than others. Animals are either predator or prey, and somewhere, someone came up with this now famous aphorism:

> *Every morning in Africa an antelope rises early and must be ready to run fast, or it will become a meal. At the same time, a lion awakens with an empty belly and also must be ready to run fast or remain hungry!*

For millions of years, our ultimate form of locomotion was walking and running. In Matobo National Park in Zimbabwe, painted on the wall of a cave is a succession of small, stick-like human figures in a clear running stride, all clutching delicate bows, quivers, and arrows. These hunters are running in one direction, from left to right, the one leading the procession has its hands thrown up in the air in the universal runners' gesture of victory. We may witness this gesture today in the modern Olympic Games. It is a natural, impulsive reaction from someone who has felt the exhilaration of victory over adversity. The image of the bushman is an iconic reminder that the roots of our running, our competitive nature, and our striving for excellence go back very far and deep.

The American Endurance Running Scene

American elite endurance runners emerge from our youth and high school programs, where thousands of young athletes begin their running careers. Furthermore, high school and collegiate programs provide the United States with a farm system second to none. So, why is it that we produce so few medal winners at the World and Olympic Games?

The problem lies in our roots. To begin with, we are a riding nation, whereas the countries that produce most of the medals emerge from walking and running societies. By walking or running to school, church, and work, or to visit relatives and play, young people in these countries develop a base for strong leg muscles. By the time they are of high school age, their working muscles are as strong as American collegiate runners. Another factor affecting this issue is the fact that when our young males decide to compete in athletic events, those with the best basic speed and athletic ability have been siphoned off into football and soccer. The same factor is true with young females with soccer and volleyball. What the cross-country coach gets is mostly the bottom of the athletic chain.

When track season rolls around, the head coach wants to determine where the talent lies in the new team. The coach then has a time trial in the 100 meter. The top four or five become sprinters; the next in line become hurdlers and jumpers, and then of course the heavyset members become throwers. The coach in charge of developing 800, 1600, and 3200 runners gets whomever is left. There are few in this group who possess good basic speed. The coach then further impedes their basic speed by sending them out to build up minutes of running with little or no instructions on proper running mechanics or any functional muscle strengthening to prepare their muscles for running.

Excerpt from the *Track & Field Omnibook:*

"I'd start jogging twice a week for five minutes – ten – twenty – thirty: then three times a week, then daily. I'd do it on a time and fun basis. … Distance runners develop primarily by a very simple process— progressive increments of enjoyable running."

This approach is the basic theory of training followed by entry level coaches throughout the U.S. The theory is to start easy and slow, then build toward faster running. Given their own means of interpreting running form, entry level athletes will, with few exceptions, develop a running rhythm that features overstriding with a slow turnover and foot strike. As the number of minutes of slow running is increased, the athlete becomes neuromuscularly adept at running slow. The slow-to-fast theory of developing entry level athletes defies the fact that speed is the most important physiological factor in determining a person's ability to race at any distance.

Somewhere during the latter part of the training season, the coach decides that in order to race, it might be necessary to develop some speed. Since it takes several weeks of specific training to improve basic speed, it is too late to be truly effective for that season. In many cases, the coach has not spent enough training time conditioning the muscles that do the work of running to withstand this new stress. As a result injury rates often rise dramatically during the last few weeks of the season.

The solution to producing better elite runners in this country is for the USATF Coaches Education Committee to come up with a training scheme in which entry-level athletes are taught to run with power and efficiency and to develop strong, fatigue-resistant working muscles. If these young hopefuls could be exposed to heavy doses of these types of activities for the first 10 years of their running development, they would be a more complete runner by the time they become emerging elite athletes. As the following quotes from the *Track & Field Omnibook* indicate, the complete runner is someone with speed and strong, fatigue-resistant working muscles that can sustain speed endurance paces for long periods of time and still be able to sprint at the end of a race:

• Basic speed is the most important single factor in 400 meter performance. There is a close relationship between 100 meter time and 400 meter time and 400 meters time with the 800, 1500, 3k, 5k, and 10k.

- Lee Evans: "Run as fast as possible while staying completely relaxed. The ultimate competitor is one who learns how to sustain an all-out fast, relaxed effort for the entire distance" (faster—looser). OK.
- In the Jim Ryan story, Coach Timmons: Jim worked for six weeks to do one thing—learn how to sprint when tired.

Haile Gebrselassie was able to use his speed to surge to a 10-meter lead, then drop back to his race pace and hold that lead. Medals in the World and Olympic Games endurance races go to the athletes who can run the fastest when fatigued. They are the best in the world because they have learned to run fast-relaxed during their development from entry level.

Learning to run fast-relaxed is a neuromuscular training procedure. Until the leaders in the profession of coaching endurance runners change their concept of the physiological aspects of developing the complete endurance athlete, the United States will never gain prominence in this area.

Until American coaches and athletes shun the myth that an individual must establish an aerobic base with sub-maximal paced running before adding other physiological aspects of training, the United States is doomed to lag behind in the world of endurance running. In order to change, our training scheme must be built around teaching our entry-level athletes how to run with power and efficiency and build strong, fatigue-resistant leg muscles. Once this is accomplished, we can jump-start all of the other physiological systems and develop both the cardiovascular and neuromuscular aspects.

The faster an athlete's 400 meter time, the greater the potential to race in endurance events, ranging from 800 meters to 10k. Improving 400 meter time should be at the top of the list when planning workouts. In order to continually improve basic speed, athletes must be taught to run with power and efficiency. This learning process must be combined with developing strong, fatigue-resistant working muscles—primarily the core, buttocks, quads and hamstrings.

The basic element of improving real speed is learning to run fast-relaxed. Clyde Hart: "In order to improve speed, you must eliminate as much backside mechanics as possible, as well as increase frontside mechanics as much as possible." Running skills must be the first thing taught to endurance runners and must be continued throughout their entire running career.

Even though Sir Mohamed Muktar Jama Farrar (renowned British distance runner) did the traditional 120 miles per week, he had to spend four years working on improving his speed before he became the best 5k-10k runner in the world. Another example is American long-distance runner Galen Rupp, who finally won a World Medal, after he spent considerable training time improving his speed.

If we accept the fact that basic speed determines an athlete's potential to race any distance, why do coaches in the USA wait until later in the season to develop this aspect? Why not make the very first step of the training period a fast one. In fact, young, unconditioned, entry-level athletes are capable of running short, fast distances from the very beginning. Short, fast intervals, accompanied by functional muscle strengthening, will form a base for all of the other physiological aspects of training. The greater the stress on the muscles, the greater the stress on the heart.

Coaches are aware of the neuromuscular aspects of training, but either do not understand this aspect or chose to ignore it. The neurological aspects of training entail learning to run with power and efficiency and engaging in specific strengthening of the muscles that do the work of running. Not only must running skills be the first thing a coach teaches an endurance running hopeful, they must be continued on a daily basis throughout the entire season, as well as the athlete's entire running career.

CHAPTER 2

Teaching Fundamental Running Skills

❑ *Posture:* A tall, relaxed torso, with the head and shoulders directly over the hips

❑ *Arms:* The arms are the key to relaxation while running. The basic element of improving speed is learning to run fast-relaxed. The arms are held at approximately a 90° angle and hang loosely from the shoulder joints. As the elbows move back and forth during the arm swing, the forearm closes the angle slightly at the top of the swing and opens slightly at the bottom of the swing. The hands are closed loosely, with the thumbnails pointing upward. There is no contraction of the muscles in the lower arms.

❑ *Foot strike:* The foot is the lever that provides force for forward movement. The foot is composed of a heel bone, tendons, ligaments, and soft tissue that provides stretch power energy that is stored during each foot strike. The foot strikes the surface slightly in front of the heel bone and slightly on the outside. As the weight of the runner's body is being supported, the foot slightly pronates and then supinates slightly as the body moves forward. The compression of the tendons and ligaments, along with the pronation and supination action of the foot, provides the force for forward motion. The further back under the center of mass the foot strike occurs, the quicker the foot strikes. The quicker the foot strike, the greater the force created.

❑ *Frontside mechanics:* When the toes push off, the thigh and knee are lifted forward and upward. As the thigh reaches its most forward and upward position, the lower leg is extended forward and then quickly brought downward to cause a foot strike to occur just in front of the heel bone and as far backwards as possible. When the foot makes contact with the surface, the knee is slightly flexed during the support phase.

❑ *Backside mechanics:* As the foot pushes backward, and the toes leave the surface, the foot must be driven upward toward the knee as soon as possible. This action will cause a high-heel follow-through, and a shorter angle between the upper and lower leg. The shorter this angle, the quicker the foot gets back onto the surface. The less time the foot spends on the surface and in the air, the faster an individual can run.

❑ *Turnover and stride length:* A turnover is every time the same foot touches down. There are two steps per turnover which are collectively referred to as a stride. The optimal turnover for efficient endurance running is 96-98 per minute. Michael Johnson, when racing the 400 meters, used a turnover of two per second. Stride length and turnover must be compatible. Stride length is determined by how far back under the center of mass the foot strike occurs. A quick turn-over with a medium length stride is most efficient. In order to accelerate running velocity, a runner should increase the turnover rate without sacrificing stride length. Trying to run faster by lengthening the stride length not only is inefficient, it will also result in greater fatigue. Running speed can only be increased when the foot strike is moving backward at a greater speed than the center of mass is moving forward.

All Gold medal winners of endurance running events in the World and Olympic Games exhibit similar running characteristics. They exhibit a tall, relaxed torso, with their head and shoulders directly over the hips. The arms move with a short, quick, forward, and backward motion. The foot strike is quick, as the foot is driven back under the center of mass. The side view of the foot cycle resembles that of a wheel. The running action exhibits a full range of motion, with an ankle-over-knee recovery. Entry-level endurance runners can be taught to emulate Gold Medal running form.

Have the athlete begin by quickstep walking with an ankle-over-ankle movement while maintaining good posture and arm action. Perform this action for 10 seconds x 6. Walk 10 seconds and then quickstep run with ankle-over-ankle foot action for 10 seconds x 6. Next, progress to 10 seconds of ankle over mid shin quickstep running, and finally to 10 seconds of ankle-over-knee running action. This progression of learning can be incorporated into the warm-up.

Teaching Gold Medal Running Form

❏ *The Foot*

The foot is the lever that provides the force for running. The contours of the foot, along with its tendons, ligaments, and toes, provide stretch-power energy for running. The foot is the end of a kinetic chain of muscles, tendons, and ligaments that begin at the core and glutes and then continue by links down through the quads, hamstrings, gastric, and Achilles tendon. All of these appendages go on stretching, as the weight of the runner's body is absorbed with each footfall. As the runner's center of mass moves in front of the foot, all of the stretch power of the kinetic chain releases energy that propels the runner's body forward.

❏ *Foot Placement*

The foot should strike the running surface just in front of the heel bone and slightly on the outer side. The farther back under the center of mass the foot lands, the quicker the foot strike. The quicker the foot strike, the greater the force created.

❏ *Teaching Foot Placement*

Running, which is controlled by the central nervous system, is a neuromuscular activity. The neuromuscular system is a human computer that can be programmed to produce specific actions. The manner in which the foot strikes the surface and its position with relation to the runner's center of mass as it strikes are important for balance and power. A balanced body, with the head and shoulders directly over the hips and a foot strike that occurs as far back under the center of mass as possible, provides the greatest power and the best economical use of a runner's energy. The neuromuscular system not only controls all muscular contractions and relaxations but also the intensity and duration of all muscular action.

Programming the Foot Strike Speed-Agility Ladder

A sure way to teach a runner proper foot placement is using a speed-agility ladder. As a rule, a speed-agility ladder is approximately 20 feet long, with rungs placed every 14 inches. To use such a ladder, start by imagining that you have a rod sticking through each ankle and then walk through the ladder by lifting the heel and stepping one ankle over the other, while flexing the toes downward. This walking action will teach the muscles to place the foot strike under the center of mass. Complete the walking action six times, while increasing the walking tempo each time through the ladder. Next, perform this action while running and increase the tempo each time.

An athlete should work toward running as fast as possible, while keeping the foot strike within the confines of the ladder rungs. To further program the feet to move faster, have the athlete progress through the ladder by stepping in and out of the ladder as fast as possible (two feet in—two feet out), while advancing through it. Next, face north and do the same quick-foot action, while advancing through the ladder laterally, returning facing south.

The quickstep run can also be done on the hash marks of a football field or by placing a flat stick a yard apart. When working in a speed-agility ladder, the athlete should practice maintaining good posture, as well as performing quick, relaxed arm movements.

Acceleration Ladder

The next step in learning the progression of running is to work in an acceleration ladder. This ladder systematically increases the stride length while, keeping the foot strike under the center of mass. For the first eight steps, use flat sticks set at 1.5', 2', 2.5', 3', 3.5', 4', 4.5', and 5' apart. For beginning runners, work up to 4' and then keep a 4' spacing, until they become adept at that stride length. For those individuals who can advance beyond a 4' stride, the settings would increase to 5' and eventually 6' (5'-3", 5'-6", 5'-9", and 6'). When a young female can run smoothly using a 5' stride, she will become an accomplished runner, as will a young male at 6'. The most effective acceleration ladder is laid out with flat sticks for the first eight strides and then with 3" risers to a distance of 30 meters, followed by utilizing 5" risers to 45 meters. The ultimate ladder advances to 60 meters using 7" risers from 45 meters to 60 meters.

The running action should be a sprint-start through the flat sticks, ankle-over-mid shin to 30 meters, and ankle-over-knee for the rest of the ladder. A 45m ladder is very practical, since the runner can continue beyond that distance using muscle memory to complete any distance desired. Remember to maintain a tall, relaxed posture, with the arms moving fast-relaxed throughout each effort.

Developing Running Velocity Without Ladders

When ladders are not available, the following progression of running can be used to instill muscle memory. To warm up, begin by walking for 10 seconds. Then perform ankle-over-ankle quickstep running for 10 seconds, followed by 10 seconds of ankle-over-mid shin running. Next, transition into an ankle-over-knee running action for 30 seconds. Continue this sequence for 10 minutes, as you continue undertaking a dynamic warm-up.

As noted previously, in order to accelerate running velocity, a runner should increase the turnover rate without shortening the stride. Trying to run faster by lengthening the stride length not only is inefficient, it also results in greater fatigue. In fact, running speed can only be increased when the foot strike is moving backward faster than the center of mass is moving forward. It should be noted that too much backside mechanics occurs when the toes finish pushing off the surface and the foot and lower leg follow-through too far behind the center of mass, causing a long leg lever for the recovery leg. This action slows the forward leg movement and causes a pronounced heel strike and braking action.

Considerable scientific evidence documents the fact that a person's basic speed is the single most important physiological variable determining a human being's ability to race at any distance. As such, 400-meter time can be used to predict a runner's performance in the 800 meters, 1500 meters, 3k, 5k, and 10k. In that regard, a formula exists for determining a runner's potential to race in those events, computing training paces based on a percentage of 400 meters speed. For example, running 400 meters in 60 seconds would yield the following calculations:

Event	Percentage	Potential Time	400 Meters Goal Pace
800	.91-.92	2:13	65
1500	.84-.85	4:28	69
3k	.77-.78	9:50	74
5k	.75-.76	16:50	79
10k	.74-.75	34:00	83
Steeple	.74-.75	10:12	83
Mile	.84-.85	4:47	69

According to the *Track & Field Omnibook*, an athlete with greater speed can carry a given pace for a short distance with a relatively lower level of stress. This factor sets the parameter for goal-pace training. Assuming equal pace, the greater the distance of each run, the greater the stress produced, even though the rest intervals are increased correspondingly. For example, 3 x 400 at 60s with 60s rest produces greater stress than 200m with 30s rest. The recovery period or the time between runs, (from a heart-strengthening standpoint), the work period, and the rest period are developmental. During the first 10 seconds of the rest period, the stress is the greatest, and, therefore, the greatest stimulus for expansion and development. The development period can last up to 30 seconds.

CHAPTER 3
The Pace

A pace that is considerably faster than race-goal pace not only achieves a developmental heart stress, it also develops a fast-twitch function in the leg muscles which, is necessary for a sustained sprint at the end. The greater the number of muscle units and fast twitch fibers recruited, the stronger the working muscles. The stronger the working muscles, the harder they can make the heart work. The stronger the heart muscle, the more oxygen rich blood being sent to the muscles that do the work of running.

When an athlete's best potential race distance has been determined, the best way to develop race potential is by training at variable paces. Variable pace training was conceived by British club coaches during the early 50s and 60s. During this time period, numerous world records were set using variable pace training.

The essence of the variable pace system is to train at race-pace plus two paces that are faster than goal-pace and two paces that are slower than race-goal pace. For example an 800 meters runner would train with sprint work and 400 meters pace, as well as paces at 1500 and 3k. These paces provide both speed effort and endurance. A greater percentage of work is done at race-goal pace because the more work done at a specific pace, the more the athlete becomes efficient at running that pace.

There are numerous theories attendant to the development of the physiological variables that are involved in training individuals to race in endurance events. Most training programs in the United States, however, concentrate on developing the cardiovascular variables of running physiology. Precious little attention is given to developing the neuromuscular aspects of training. Over time, coaches and endurance runners adopted a scheme of training that is presented as the only way to physiological development.

Ultimately coaches and athletes have become satisfied with the result of a training scheme that focuses strictly on cardiovascular enhancements. Any neuromuscular power that does develop is through the act of running alone, with little to no help from functional muscle strengthening activities, which will produce a complete runner if practiced.

Subsequently, many runners defined the various physiological variables that are involved in training to compete in endurance racing. These physiological variables are divided into two categories: cardiovascular and neuromuscular. The cardio variables are $\dot{V}O_2max$, $v\dot{V}O_2max$, lactate threshold, and general endurance. The neuromuscular variables are functional strength, running economy, speed, and muscular power. In reality, two runners that are the same size and with equal $\dot{V}O_2max$ will seldom finish a race at the same time, because one of them would most likely have better running economy or possess greater basic speed.

The brain initiates running and the actions of the neuromuscular system, which stimulates contraction. Conditioning the brain to allow us to run at higher velocities will lead to better race performance. The heart and lungs remain at their resting rate until stimulated by a demand for oxygen, which is created through muscle contractions.

The intensity and duration of contractions determine how fast and how long the heart must accelerate its rate of work in order to supply the amount of oxygen demanded. The strength of the heart muscle is limited by the extent to which the duration and intensity of a muscle contraction occurs. The duration and intensity of muscle contractions are limited by the strength and power of the muscles to perform the work of running.

In reality, the heart, lungs and circulatory system are dependent upon the strength and power of the working muscle for their strength and functionality. Continuous muscle contraction not only requires more oxygen, that need for oxygen alerts the brain, which signals the heart to beat faster and harder in order to supply this new demand. In the simplest terms, running is first of all a neural thing and a cardiopulmonary thing second.

To put it another way, when the heart and circulatory systems deliver oxygen and nutrients to the neuromuscular system, it is because the central nervous system first signals them to do so. The brain is the boss. The fact is that the functional strengthening of the muscles that do the work of running, along with running-skill drills, will produce increased speed and better use of energy. With a solid foundation of neuromuscular training, coordinated with multi-tiered velocities of running, every athlete will progressively raise their fitness level.

Fatigue does not begin in the muscles, but rather in the brain. The burning sensation felt at the end of an exhausting race or workout does not begin when the muscles run out of fuel, but rather when the brain tells the muscles to conserve energy. Muscle biopsies taken at the end of a marathon show that there is plenty of fuel (ATP) for muscular contractions still available. The brain, however, has signaled to the runner to conserve energy for self-preservation purposes.

Every runner has an innate amount of energy reserves. If your brain does not know how much energy you will need for a specific effort, such as a hard race, it will error on the side of caution and tell you to shut down. As a runner, you need to rewire your brain to believe that your muscles can continue to push. To be successful at this, you must envision it. In that regard, it can be helpful to repeat to yourself, "I am strong and swift" during difficult workouts or races.

There is no doubt an aerobic base must be established to become an accomplished endurance runner. Arthur Lydiard, the world-renowned distance coach from New Zealand, developed several Olympic medal winners. In his training regimens, 100-mile training weeks became the norm. Nowhere in Lydiard's coaching efforts, however, did he claim that speed development could not be a part of the training scheme from the very beginning. To quote Lydiard: "If you want to be a successful runner, you have to consider everything. It is not good just to be thinking about endurance and not develop fine speed. You have to take a long view and train on all aspects of development through a systematic program. We had to obtain the best possible results in a limited time, and the best way to develop aerobic capacity was to train at higher aerobic speeds."

Contrary to popular belief, running intervals do not actually improve speed. Repetitions of intervals result in improved mechanics and create a high oxygen debt to develop a buffer against fatigue, which allows a runner to hold their top running velocity for a longer period. Eventually though, the runner will tighten up and not be able to relax, causing their muscles to shut down. In order to develop speed, a runner must remain fresh and relaxed and avoid tightening up.

If runners in the United States expect to improve enough to become competitive in the worldwide endurance racing, coaches must begin developing the neuromuscular variable of running concurrently with the cardio aspects at the entry level. If all endurance athletes were exposed to a concentrated program of running skills, functional leg strengthening, and speed development for the entire training season and continuing over their running career, they would be prepared to compete at their best.

Whether the race entails 100 meters, or 10k, it is a foot race, in which it is the act of running that brings the torso to the finish line. It is the act of running that causes the heart to work at intensities high enough to bring about improvements in the cardiovascular system's ability to deliver oxygen-rich blood to the muscles and organs that do the work of running.

The act of running is a neuromuscular issue, which is controlled by the central nervous system. The central nervous system consists of the brain, the spinal cord, and all of the nerves that stimulate muscular contractions. It is the neuromuscular system that controls the power for running and determines the efficiency with which fuel is used.

CHAPTER 4 ━━━━━━━━━━━

The Race

In essence, a running race is a foot race. Running a race of any distance is done by the foot striking the running surface. As the foot makes contact, all of the kinetic chain goes on stretch, storing kinetic energy amounting to approximately 2.5 times the runner's weight. The kinetic chain consists of all the muscles, tendons, and ligaments—from the toes to the buttock muscles.

When the center of mass is directly over the foot, the stretch-shortening cycle comes into play. During the stretch-shortening cycle, muscles first stretch (pre-activated) and then recoil, producing with each snap back the propulsive force that moves the body forward. The muscles stiffness or tenacity of the muscles plays a significant role in determining the amount of energy stored and snap back ability.

Studies indicate that running-specific strengthening activities greatly enhance the stretch-shortening cycle phenomenon. As the runner extends the length of the run or increases the intensity of the run, the kinetic chain will begin to fatigue, because the resistance to stretching may decrease force production. This situation occurs because less energy is stored in the reverse spring with each touchdown, which, in turn, may result in a diminishing stride length due to the push-off stage being elongated, thereby releasing less energy.

The nervous system is required to coordinate and direct leg muscles in a more powerful way in order for faster running to occur. Maximal speed occurs when the neuromuscular system learns to promote faster stride rates, shorter contact with the ground per step, and quicker generation of propulsive force. The quicker the foot gets off the ground and returns, the more force created by each touchdown. The neuromuscular system can be programmed to produce these actions through teaching running skills that bring about proper frontside and backside mechanics.

A key goal for endurance athletes is to develop the ability to run more quickly by expanding the capacity to sustain higher speeds over extended periods of time. It is the act of running that stimulates the heart to work at a higher rate, which improves stroke volume, creates more capillaries to carry oxygen to each cell, and increases the number and size of mitochondria, as well as the density of mitochondrial enzymes. Any running, regardless of form, will jump start the runner's $\dot{V}O_2$max and lactate-conversion processes. On the other hand, if a person wants to compete in endurance races they must learn how to run with the correct frontside and backside mechanics, while maintaining the correct posture, relaxing the upper body, and performing the arm movement. Foot strike, turn-over, and stride length must be instilled into the neuromuscular system through running-skill drills.

Beginning runners, as well as those runners with some experience and elite athletes, all have the same needs in order to improve their race performance. Learning to run with power and how to use muscle fuel efficiently is the number one training priority to race at any distance. In order for any athlete to run with power and efficiency for an extended length of time, they must develop strong fatigue-resistant muscle strength. This objective is best accomplished by performing running-specific strength exercises.

An athlete's basic speed is the single most important physiological variable in determining their ability to compete at any distance. Speed = stride rate X stride length. The perfect combination of these two variables is the goal of the rhythm of running. If coaches periodize their training scheme and focus on teaching running skills, running specific muscle strengthening and improving basic speed, $\dot{V}O_2$max and lactate threshold will be developed concurrently.

Running a race of any distance is, first and foremost, a neuromuscular issue with cardiovascular activity being secondary. In fact, foot-strike time, turnover rate, and stride length are greater detriments of the racing potential of an endurance runner than are the cardiovascular variables. The neuromuscular system consists of the brain, spinal cord, and nerves that control all muscular actions.

The brain is the center for all movement that occurs in human beings. The brain controls the intensity and duration of each muscle contraction and coordinates the contraction and relaxation of each muscle fiber. Any muscular contraction will cause the heart to work at the intensity necessary to send sufficient oxygen to produce the energy needed. This factor is controlled by the brain. The brain can be trained to bring about desired actions that can produce power and efficiency in a person's running—a goal that can be accomplished through skill work and a series of running-specific strengthening exercises.

Running begins with the foot applying force to the running surface. The quicker the foot gets on and off the surface, the more force created with each touchdown. The quicker the foot is cycled through for the next strike, the greater the economy of fuel expended. The heart and lungs provide the fuel for the muscles to move the body forward, but it is the economical use of energy and power production of the muscles that is the essence of racing in endurance events. The heart and lungs go along for the ride while the muscles are bringing the torso to the finish line.

Several documented studies indicate that the best approach to planning a training scheme is through the development of running skills, running-specific strengthening, and the improvement of basic speed. An athlete's basic speed is the physiological variable that most determines their potential to race at any distance. Training to race in any event is simply a matter of training the neuromuscular system to produce proper running skills, fatigue-resistant muscle strength, and power for greater speed.

Periodization of training to race should be based on the S.S.S. concept. If an individual cannot run with power and efficiency, all of the other physiological variables are negated in their capacity to produce race results.

A person's $\dot{V}O_2$max rating (amount of oxygen available to make fuel) is not the best indicator of their ability to race in endurance events. For example, Frank Shorter's $\dot{V}O_2$max was a mere 70 milliliters of oxygen per kg of body weight per 60 seconds. Steve Prefontaine's was 86. The average elite Kenyan has an 86 $\dot{V}O_2$max.

So what makes one runner faster than another? Perhaps the best Kenyan runners are the individuals who ran the most miles to school in their youth. The average elite Kenyan athlete has a cruising turnover rate of 98 per minute. Steve Scott, Bob Kennedy, and Steve Prefontaine all were at 96 turnovers per minute. If the average stride length, when racing, is 7'6", a turnover of 98 versus 96 would put that runner ahead by approximately five meters each minute.

Numerous studies support the fact that a male with a $\dot{V}O_2$max of 70 or greater can create adequate energy to become a world champion. The fact that a man with a $\dot{V}O_2$max of 70 can beat runners with higher ratings can be attributed to the fact that either the individual's running mechanics are more efficient or that person has greater basic speed. If a training scheme is created, based on teaching efficient running mechanics, creating more power with each foot strike, and promoting fatigue resistant muscular strength, $\dot{V}O_2$max, and LTRV can concurrently be developed to the fullest.

Anaerobic energy is produced before any aerobic energy enters the energy continuum. Speed work recruits the maximum number of fast-twitch fibers. The contraction of fast-twitch fibers produces power which translates to speed. High-intensity sprint training produces two key adaptions that are beneficial to endurance runners—a reduced rate of oxygen usage and a smaller buildup of lactate. Ten minutes of running at 100 percent $\dot{V}O_2$max roughly triples aerobic enzymes. Even beginning runners can safely do short segments of speed work.

Teaching athletes to run fast-relaxed should be the basic fundamental of any training scheme. Running fast-relaxed for short segments and then extending the length of the segment, while staying completely relaxed, will cause the heart to beat faster and pump more blood per contraction, thereby improving stroke volume. The stronger the working muscles, the stronger the heart muscle and vice versa. A healthy heart muscle cannot be damaged by intensity of work, because it receives all of the oxygen needed to withstand any effort, before the oxygen is passed on to the other muscles.

To ensure the greatest race performance, high-intensity running is a must. In order to complete volumes of intense running, the muscles must be strengthened to withstand the stress. The neuromuscular system must receive equal training time comparable to what the cardiovascular system experiences. Scientific research indicates that not only will $\dot{V}O_2$max and muscle fibers adapt to systematic increases in intensity and volume, it will also improve in strength for a period of about 21 days. It will then need approximately seven days of training at less intensity, before rebuilding to a higher level.

These factors make a training scheme of 28 days a logical training period. A training plan of 16 weeks fits most seasons of competitions. Evidence suggests that work for the first four to six weeks of training should concentrate on forming a base for improving both basic speed and running-specific muscle strengthening, while jump starting the improvement of $\dot{V}O_2$max and the ability to convert lactate back to energy.

America's elite athletes are products of our youth, high school, and collegiate track and cross country programs. If we could expose our entry-level hopefuls to a training scheme that teaches the learning of running skills, the strengthening of the muscles that do the work of running, and the development of basic speed and then to continue this plan for the first 10 years of their development, America could produce athletes who could be able to compete with elite athletes throughout the world. Competition in this country consists of two seasons—cross country and track. The training and competition season for youth and high school athletes typically lasts for 16 weeks, with collegiate and elite seasons somewhat longer. In fact, all endurance runners have the same needs regardless of age or ability levels, including the following:

- Learn to run with power and efficiency.
- Learn to hold the fastest pace possible for the longest possible time.
- Develop strong fatigue-resistant working muscles.
- Develop the highest $\dot{V}O_2$max rating possible.
- Improve the ability of the muscles to convert lactate to ATP.
- Train the brain to withstand the highest pain level possible.

The typical high school, 16-week program for cross country and track can serve as a model. Other levels of competition can make adjustments, according to age or ability levels. Competition plays a vital role in the overall training scheme. An endurance race would be considered a $\dot{V}O_2$max workout. While a relatively easy workout day can be scheduled the day prior to the race, athletes should only taper for their most important races.

For our model, we can use a five-day work week. Races and additional workdays might make up a sixth or seventh day. Divide the training and racing season into 28-day segments. Allow 21 days of exposure to progressively increasing intensity and volume and seven days of less stressful work to allow the body to adjust. This scheduling follows the principle of muscle fiber and $\dot{V}O_2$max strength improvement. Peaking is an everyday process and coincides with raising an individual's level of fitness. Fitness levels are highest during the seven days of less stressful work. Races can be scheduled accordingly.

During the first four to six weeks of training, we should concentrate on developing a base for power and speed, while jump starting the $\dot{V}O_2$max and lactate conversion processes. Running is a neuromuscular activity first and a cardio activity second. No aerobic activity occurs until some anaerobic activity takes place.

Planning Daily, Weekly, and Seasonal Workouts

Numerous studies leave no doubt that a runner's basic level of speed is the single physiological variable that most determines a person's potential to race at any distance. A person's basic speed is determined by their ability to produce power with each foot strike, which is accomplished through running mechanics that causes the foot strike to be a quick-off and back-on the running surface.

The nervous system's role in speed development is independent of the energy-producing systems within the muscles. Any running, regardless of technique, will stimulate the heart to beat faster in an effort to deliver the required amount of oxygen for the production of enough fuel to allow the running to occur. The running action activates the neuromuscular and cardiovascular systems concurrently.

Any training scheme to race in endurance events must take into consideration that these two systems are entwined and that one depends on the other for improvement. The structure of the daily workout begins with a warm-up that consists of running skills, overall body-strengthening activities, and running-specific strength exercises. The workout should then continue with running segments that are specific to developing speed, lactate conversion, and $\dot{V}O_2$max. This continuous workout lasts from 60 to 90 minutes. The workout concludes with a 15-minute cool-down, featuring running-specific strengthening exercises, stretching, striding forward and backward, crazy feet, plank core, eccentric reaches, and stretching the I.T. band, quads and hamstrings.

The first four weeks of training is dedicated to teaching running skills that produce powerful and efficient running. Exercises should be performed that develop fatigue-resistant muscle strength. In addition, a base for improving basic speed should be established. Running workouts should concentrate on developing the athlete's 400 meters speed. An endurance runner's basic speed is measured by their 400 meters time. As such, 400 meters work jump-starts the $\dot{V}O_2$max and lactate conversion systems.

Quality vs. Quantity

More and more scientific evidence is being published that favors quality over quantity in developing the ability of endurance runners to race in distances of 800 meters and up. A review of the workouts of elite runners throughout the world shows that while the "best of the best" do more quality work in their training, the world champions only average about 13 percent quality in their training.

Considerable research points to the fact that the periodization of training to race distances of 800 meters to 10k should be based on the development of skill, speed, and strength. Speed and strength are far better indicators of an individual's potential to race in these events than are endurance factors, such as $\dot{V}O_2max$.

In that regard, workouts emphasizing skill, speed, and strength should be performed that address the following factors:

- Learn how to run with power and efficiency.
- Learn how to run fast-relaxed.
- Learn how to hold the fastest pace possible for as long as possible.
- Learn how to hold a specific race pace for as close to race distance as possible.
- Develop strong fatigue resistant muscles through running specific muscle strengthening.

When all of the aforementioned are put into place, speed, speed endurance, $v\dot{V}O_2max$, $\dot{V}O_2max$, and LTRV will concurrently be developed to the maximum.

Guidelines for Planning a Training Season to Develop the Complete Runner

- Always start with a dynamic warm-up and end with a dynamic cool-down.
- Start off with short segments of running, while working on gold medal running form. Develop a quick-foot strike and a turnover rate of 98 per minute.
- Use circuit training as basis for lactate threshold running economy and overall body strength.
- Work on speed enhancement every day.
- Begin building an endurance base by using fartlek-type workouts
- Gradually increase the length of runs, while checking turnover frequently.
- At the end of eight weeks, do the six-minute run test to determine the runner's $v\dot{V}O_2max$ and $\dot{V}O_2max$ fitness levels.
- Calculate training paces for goal-pace interval work.
- Use $v\dot{V}O_2max$ paces for interval work to improve maximum oxygen up take. Upgrade the paces as the runner's race performance improves.
- Train at race-goal paces that are both faster and slower than the individual's preferred race distance. Utilize multi-tiered training paces.
- Design daily workouts to accomplish a specific training goal. Let the mileage run be a result of carefully planned workouts, not a set quota.
- Run barefoot, whenever possible.

Guidelines for the Beginning of the Season

- Begin every workout with a dynamic warm-up that features running skills and functional muscle-strengthening activities.

- Use short segments of running, while working on foot strike and turnover.
- Employ short reps to learn how to relax while running.
- Initiate high levels of lactate for numerous short periods of time.
- Incorporate speed development drills.
- Use fartlek-type work to develop $\dot{V}O_2max$.
- After six weeks of practice—give six-minute run test for $v\dot{V}O_2max$.
- Run intervals of 30 seconds to three minutes at $v\dot{V}O_2max$ with 1:1 rest. Example: 5 x 30 secs @ 5M/PS = 750 meters.
- Use variable paces for interval work, including segments at 800 meters, 1500 meters, 3k, 5k, and 10k effort.

The Basis for Training to Race in Endurance Events

While the heart and lungs produce the energy for running endurance races, it is how the muscles use this energy that determines race results. The strength and fatigue-resistance of the muscles determines the extent to which the heart and lungs can be made to work. The brain is in control of all of these physiological functions. The brain can be programmed to produce power, running efficiency, and pain tolerance.

Training Blocks

$\dot{V}O_2max$ and muscle fibers will improve in strength when exposed to increased intensity and volume for a period of about 21 days. They then need about seven days of training at less intensity and volume to adjust and be ready for the next 21 days of slightly more intense work. This 28-day block of training can easily be inserted into the entire training scheme. An endurance runner's fitness level will be the highest during the seven days of lesser work. As such, important races can be scheduled accordingly.

Quality

Quality work is synonymous with speed work. Speed work for endurance runners is defined as 10k race pace or faster. 10k pace would be speed work for the half marathon; 5k for the 10k; 3k for the 5k; 1500 for the 3k; 800 for the 1500; 400 for the 800; and sprints for the 400. Quality work is limited by the ability of the neuromuscular system to maintain a specified pace for extended periods of time. Running-specific strength determines an individual's fatigue-resistant level.

An athlete's ability to do a higher percentage of quality work is greatly enhanced by running skills that produce proper frontside and backside mechanics, along with fatigue-resistant muscle strength. Running skills should be developed that produce a full range of motion, with a foot strike that occurs under the athlete's center of mass.

Such a footstrike enables the individual to get off the ground quickly, with a high heel follow-through that forms a short angle between the thigh and calf that allows the foot to return to the running surface as quickly as possible.

Running Economy and Running Efficiency

Running economy is the energy cost of running at a fixed speed. Running efficiency is the ratio of work performed to energy expended. Improving these physiological variables involves training that improves the ability to run faster while using the same internal oxygen-delivery system ($\dot{V}O_2$max).

Running intervals at the pace determined by the six-minute run test, with 1:1 easy running rest, along with 1500 meters + 3k goal-pace running velocities, will produce optimal use of energy. These are paces where stride rate and stride length are in perfect harmony. Learning to run with a stride rate of 96 to 98 turnovers per minute, causing the foot strike to occur underneath the center of mass, will produce a runner's optimal efficient use of muscle fuel.

Another aspect of improving running economy is strengthening the muscles that do the work of running through running-specific strengthening exercises. These exercises mimic some phase of the stride gait and improve the ability of the kinetic chain to produce stretch power. Running-specific strengthening exercises involve using an individual's own bodyweight as the resistance factor. Doing strengthening exercises, while mimicking some phase of the stride gate, not only improves muscle strength, it also makes the muscles more fatigue-resistant. Running-Specific strengthening exercises can easily be incorporated into the warm-up and cool-down, as well as be performed as part of a circuit.

The Fundamentals of Training to Race in Endurance Events

Ask any successful football or basketball coach, *"What is your secret of success?"* The answer will invariably be, *"We pay attention to developing the fundamentals of the game."* On the other hand, ask a successful coach of endurance runners the same question, and the answer most likely will be, *"Run as many miles as possible and develop the cardiovascular system to its fullest extent."*

Developing a strong oxygen delivery system is certainly a basic fundamental to an endurance runner's training scheme. It is not, however, all-exclusive, as many coaches believe. Over the past several decades, American coaches of endurance athletes have been brainwashed into thinking that developing a higher $\dot{V}O_2$max rating must be done before any of the other fundamental physiological variables of training are introduced.

Typically, ascertaining the $\dot{V}O_2$max is determined through volumes of miles run at moderate paces. The theory is that beginning a training season with running slow mileage, the muscles that do the work of running will gradually increase in strength as volume increases, thus allowing the athlete to eventually run the mileage at a faster pace. In reality, this outcome does not happen, since the muscle fibers are not stressed enough to make the adaptation to provide adequate power.

In order to develop the complete runner, coaches must teach the skills of running mechanics and incorporate running-specific strengthening activities concurrently with building an aerobic base. Unless running skills are developed early, most athletes establish a stride cycle that is too elongated with a slow on-and-off-the-surface foot strike. The assumption is that as base mileage builds, the muscles that do the work of running will become stronger.

The main problem with this theory is that while running sub-maximal velocities, neuromuscular patterns are established that are not conducive to racing. Running sub-maximal velocities recruits mostly slow-twitch muscle fibers, which does not prepare the muscles for race-training velocities. Adding speed work later in the season does not allow enough time to integrate the appropriate amount of speed training to become reactive in the neuromuscular system.

Since speed is the most significant physiological variable in determining a person's ability to race at any distance, it would behoove coaches and athletes to develop this factor at the onset of the season. If we could develop speed and learn to run with power and efficiency, all of the other physiological aspects of training would fall into place. By systemically teaching a runner to hold a fast pace for progressively longer periods of time, we can jump-start all of the other variables of training.

Running fast alerts the brain to speed up the heart to supply more oxygen-rich blood to the working muscles. When this demand cannot be met fast enough, the lactate-shuttle system is activated. The lactate-shuttle system converts pyruvic acid back to ATP, making energy for continuous running. Activating the lactate shuttle system at the onset of the training season paves the way to better oxygen consumption and higher LTRV (lactate threshold running velocity) later, when major races come into the schedule.

The reality is that sub-maximal running velocities do not recruit enough muscle units to significantly improve leg muscle strength. Furthermore, running sub-maximal velocities for extended periods of time retards basic speed, because no fast twitch fibers are recruited, and neuromuscular patterns are established that produce a slow turn-over and foot strike.

Before developing a training scheme to run a foot race of any distance, coaches and athletes should consider what it takes to develop the complete competitor. They should first define the physiological fundamentals that are involved in such a tremendous task. By examining scientific research and reviewing successful training schemes that have produced Olympic and world champions, we can define the fundamentals of training to race in endurance events at 800 meters and longer, which include the following:

- *Running with proper biomechanics:* In races of any distance, it is the act of running that brings the torso to the finish line. The manner in which the runner executes the act of running determines their ability to hold a fast race-pace, answer opponent's surges during the race, and respond to the closing speed of other competitors.

- *Maximum neuromuscular power:* The greater your maximal running velocity, the higher your performance speed in endurance events will be. As your basic running speed increases, your time in the 800 through the marathon will improve, partially because your previous pace in these races will be easier for your neuromuscular system to handle. Recent scientific studies show a definite linkage with raw power and aerobic performance.

- *Develop strong, fatigue-resistant muscle strength:* Develop running-specific muscle strength so that your injury risk is as low as possible, fatigue-resistance is as high as it can be, and the foundation for speed improvements is established. Overall body strengthening can best be administered through functional muscle strengthening. Train the muscles to put more force on the ground with each step by using strength activities that mimic the act of running.

- *The greatest possible enhancement of the economy of movement:* It is essential that competition-specific speeds are completed at the lowest fraction of maximal energy cost or max aerobic capacity. Running economy, which is a great predictor of racing potential, is like getting the most mileage out of a tank of gas. The efficiency with which you use aerobic and anaerobic energy allows you to move up to higher running velocities during both training and racing.

- *Improving maximum oxygen uptake:* Improving the heart and capillary system's ability to supply oxygen to the mitochondria, where the aerobic power is produced is an absolute must. The best pace to run that will strengthen the heart muscle and capillary systems is $v\dot{V}O_2max$ pace, which is the minimal running velocity at which maximal aerobic capacity is attained. $v\dot{V}O_2max$ reveals the magnitude of your aerobic capacity as you run, as well as the efficiency with which you move when running at very high speeds. $v\dot{V}O_2max$ has proven to be one of the most important predictors of a person's potential to race in endurance events. On the flip side, $\dot{V}O_2max$ sets the parameter for determining lactate threshold running velocity and running efficiency, but is not the best predictor of racing potential. Two athletes with the same $\dot{V}O_2max$ will seldom finish a race at the same time. Because one individual will possess greater speed, running efficiency, or LTRV, that runner will finish first.

- *Lactate threshold running velocity:* Glycolysis is the process by which oxygen and fuel from food produces energy for muscular action. It is the byproduct of glycolysis, lactate (lactic acid), however, that produces power for continued muscular activity. As you increase the velocity of running, lactate begins to build up in the blood. When the concentration of lactate builds up to the degree that the lactate shuttle cannot convert it back to ATP, the muscles begin to shut down. The running velocity at which this situation occurs is called a person's lactate threshold running velocity (LTRV). Since lactate is a great muscular fuel, lactate threshold running velocity is like a barometer of muscle function during exercise. If lactate spills from your muscles into your blood stream at low running velocities, you are not prepared for high quality efforts. If lactate does not pool in your blood until you reach very high speeds, your muscles are doing an excellent job of converting lactate back to ATP.

❑ *Psychological preparation for racing:* Continually push your body to the highest level of intensity and pain in practice sessions, so that negative thoughts and mental restraints do not limit your efforts. Test yourself periodically to determine your fitness level and have the confidence to race at that level.

❑ *Specific race preparation:* Optimize all of the fundamentals of training and schedule important races to coincide with a rise in your fitness level. When you have determined your best potential race distance, you must run several workouts at your present race-pace and your ultimately targeted race-pace. The more running that you do at paces that coincide with your race-pace, the more efficient you become at that pace. A person's basic speed, running efficiency, and LTRV are great predictors of racing potential. The production of neuromuscular power is equally important to racing, as is cardio-power. Neuromuscular power is developed through functional muscle strengthening, speed work and economical mechanics. Having a strong heart and a well-developed capillary system is only one half of the equation for determining racing potential. If a runner cannot create the force necessary to run fast for long periods of time and then produce even more force during the critical phases of a race, they cannot become as good as they could possibly be.

The muscles that do the work of running, along with all the organs involved, are made up of specific types of muscle cells. The heart, lungs, capillaries, and skeletal muscles are composed of muscle cells that respond to training. All muscle cells respond to the stress and adaptation phenomenon (Hans Selye's general adaptation syndrome). Muscle cells combine to make up fibers that provide the tensile strength for running. When muscles are stressed beyond their present capacity, a signal is sent to the brain that is interpreted as pain. Not liking pain, the muscles adapt to this level of stress and become stronger in the process.

As coaches, we can use this phenomenon of stress and adaptation of muscle cells to plan our training scheme. We can periodize our training, based on strength and speed, and logically address all of the physiological variables in a sequence that will develop the complete runner.

All muscular actions and reactions are controlled by the neuromuscular system. Training to race in endurance events involves the development of both the cardiovascular and the neuromuscular systems. These systems must be developed concurrently in order to develop the complete runner.

If we base our periodization on systematically enhancing strength and speed, not only can we intelligently take advantage of the stress and adaptation phenomenon of muscular activity, we can also consistently improve our level of fitness. Science suggests that all of the physiological variables can gain strength through approximately 21 days and then tend to level off for seven days or so before starting a new strength cycle. A training period of 28 days gives us 21 days of an upswing in fitness with six or seven days to recover before pushing the intensity and volume to another level. During a competitive season, endurance athletes will perform best during an upswing in fitness. With this factor in mind, coaches can schedule important races to coincide with the training schedule of their athletes. Furthermore, if we expose our entry-level endurance athletes to a training scheme that promotes both cardiovascular power and neuromuscular power concurrently during their first 10 years of development, those who reach elite status will be better able to cope with elite athletes from other nations.

Running is possible, because muscular power creates energy to make muscles contract and relax. Energy to create muscular contractions is created through chemical reactions involving the food we consume and the oxygen delivered to the cells by way of the circulatory system.

Three Unique and Distinct Series of Chemical Reactions

The body has three systems by which it produces energy from ATP, the immediate usable form of chemical energy that is utilized for all cellular function. Because the body does not store a significant amount of ATP and needs a continuous supply, it must be constantly resynthesized, which it does in several ways, employing one of the following three energy systems:

❑ *ATP-PC system:* This energy system, which utilizes creatine phosphate (CV), has a very rapid rate of ATP production. The CP is used to reconstitute ATP after it is broken down to release its energy. The production of energy is instantaneous, but depletes in about 8 to 10 seconds. No assimilated oxygen is used in metabolizing the creatine phosphate. This energy system is used in short-term, high-intensity activities, such as sprinting, pole vaulting, high jumping, and long jumping.

❑ *Anaerobic glycolysis:* This pathway involves the breakdown of carbohydrates (glucose and glycogen) within muscle cells to form pyruvic acid, commonly referred to as lactic acid. No ingested oxygen is required for this energy pathway and it provides instant energy for 10 to 120 seconds. This system is the major source of energy for competing in running events, from 100 to 800 meters.

❑ *Aerobic glycolysis system:* It takes about two minutes of continuous exertion for the ATP-PC and anaerobic glycogenic system to use up stored energy and for the flow of oxygen to the muscle cells to start producing ATP. Oxygen is required for most of the cellular energy (ATP) produced by the body. Although aerobic glycolysis is the slowest way to resynthesize ATP, this energy system produces approximately 18 times more ATP than does anaerobic glycolysis. As such, aerobic glycolysis provide the energy the body requires in races that last longer than two minutes.

The three energy systems form an energy continuum that provides instant energy and allows athletes to run at fast velocities, medium-fast velocities, and not-quite-so-fast velocities, without having to stop and regenerate energy. A training scheme for training athletes to race endurance events must allow for the improvement of all three energy systems in order to produce the complete runner. The complete runner is an individual who can hold a fast pace, match surges throughout a race, and sprint with opponents during the final stage of a race.

A training scheme must provide for workouts that develop all of the physiological variables not just those that promote greater cardio power. Workouts that last from 10 seconds to two minutes and longer than two minutes must be systematically integrated into the overall scheme. The neuromuscular variables cannot be ignored in this scheme because endurance running is as much a neural thing as it is a cardio issue.

Planning workouts to develop the complete endurance athlete can be a complicated task, given that distances of 800 meters, 1500 meters, 3k, 5k, 10k and marathon are recognized as basic competitive distances for endurance racers. Competitors in any of these distances must incorporate all of the physiological fundamentals of training in order to become a complete competitor. Running speed, efficiency, and fatigue-resistant muscle strength must be developed concurrently with VO_2max and the lactate shuttle system. Coaches and athletes must decide what workouts to do, as well as in what sequence in which such workouts should be inserted in the periodization of training.

It should be emphasized that training to race at any distance is a matter of stressing muscle fibers and then allowing them to rest and adapt to a particular level of stress. If we periodize our training, based on improving speed and strength, we can systematically develop all of the cardiovascular and neuromuscular variables of training.

Many coaches in the United States and most of the Western Hemisphere are totally dedicated to developing VO_2max by adhering to the performance of mileage quota of easy-to-moderate running velocities, before adding any of the other training fundamentals to their scheme. On the other hand, Italian coach Renata Conova, who developed Olympic marathon champions Gelando Borden and Stefano Baldine (as well as coaching numerous elite runners from Kenya), does not follow this thinking. He does not start his training season by building an aerobic base, but rather by building strength and explosive muscular actions. Hill work and short, fast intervals prevail in the first few weeks of the training prescribed by Conova. Furthermore, young Kenyan hopefuls train at lactate threshold running velocities early in their development.

It should be noted that an individual's VO_2max is not a good predictor of someone's racing potential. In fact, science has proven that a person's basic speed is the best determiner of racing potential. As such, why not begin a training season by first developing speed and muscular strength? Workouts that enhance these two variables also jump-start VO_2max, LTRV, and running economy.

Coaches who periodize their training season by improving strength and speed can break the season into five categories:

- ❑ *Category #1:* Athletes should be taught to run with power and efficiency. This process should begin with developing proper frontside and backside mechanics. As this task is being done, the athlete learns to run fast-relaxed for short segments. Next, the length of each segment that can be completed fast-relaxed should be extended. If hills are available, running short, steep inclines at all-out fast-relaxed effort will add power to the working muscles. Running gradually inclining hills at a 5k effort in three-minute segments, with 1:1 rest, adds strength to the working muscles, as well as improving $\dot{V}O_2max$ and the lactate shuttle system. Hill running can also make athletes tougher psychologically, when they continue to push the pain barrier higher and higher.

- ❑ *Category #2:* Running specific strengthening workouts, consisting of resistance exercises that mimic the biomechanics of running, will not only add more force to the ground with each step, they will also condition the muscles to become more fatigue-resistant. The working muscles must be strengthened throughout the entire training and racing season, so that the highest percentage of quality work possible can be done. Combining running segments and functional strengthening activities into a circuit workout will upgrade overall strength and conditioning and, thus, improve efficiency.

  Circuit workouts create copious amounts of lactate and, in most cases, escalate oxygen consumption right up to $\dot{V}O_2max$, thereby improving LTRV and $v\dot{V}O_2max$. Circuit workouts also improve power and psychological toughness. Coaches can create speed circuits, $\dot{V}O_2max$ circuits, and marathon circuits by combining a variety of running velocities with five or six whole-body strengthening exercises. Circuit workouts entail a continuous, non-stop workout that can be upgraded as the athlete's fitness level rises.

  Running-specific strengthening workouts, consisting of resistance exercises that mimic the biomechanics of running, help athletes apply more force to the ground with each foot strike. Running-specific resistance workouts not only improve speed, they also provide potential for greater power and $v\dot{V}O_2max$ and LTRV. Runners who carry out running-specific resistance workouts feel stronger, more balanced, and more fatigue-resistant when they run. Running-specific strengthening workouts can be readily incorporated into the warm-up and cool-down sessions.

- ❑ *Category #3:* Maximum oxygen uptake and LTRV should be developed to the fullest extent. $v\dot{V}O_2max$ is the ultimate pace to train to improve $\dot{V}O_2max$. Individuals can establish their present $v\dot{V}O_2max$ running velocity by running as far as possible in six minutes. They should then divide the distance covered by six to determine how many meters they traveled per minute. The resultant number will be their $v\dot{V}O_2max$ running velocity. Athletes begin $v\dot{V}O_2max$ training by running 30-second segments, with 1:1 rest. As their fitness improves, they should systematically work up to 3.5 minutes with 1:1 rest. When doing 30-second to 60-second segments, they should complete as many segments as possible before fatiguing. For longer segments, complete 3000 of running at vVO$_2$max. vVO$_2$max workouts provide the physiological stress needed to address many of the fundamentals of training.

❑ *Category #4:* Race-specific training. The more athletes train at goal pace, the more efficient their neuromuscular system becomes at continuing that pace for longer periods of time. In order to continue to improve race times, they must also run at velocities that are faster than race-pace and some that are slower than race-pace, so that they can improve their basic speed and endurance. For example, if an individual is an 800 meters specialist, they would need to run some true speed and 400 meters velocities to improve running power, as well as their efforts at 1500 meters and 3k, in order to develop greater speed endurance. This system, called multi-tiered training, was developed by British Club coaches in the 1940s and 1950s. In fact, numerous world records have been set by British Club members, using this system.

❑ *Category #5:* Tapering. Reducing volume and adding real speed about 10 days prior to the most important races of the season is a must for optimal performance. Rest and running rhythm is of the utmost importance at this time. The last excruciatingly hard workout should be conducted about 10 days prior to the climax of the season and coincide with the end of the 21-day stress cycle. After this point, the volume of training should be reduced by 30 percent or more, but the intensity of the training should be maintained. Rest about 48 hours prior to race day, performing only a few rhythm reps at 3k pace, should suffice.

The Lactate Ladder Workouts

Lactate ladder workouts consist of running velocities that initiate high levels of aerobic glycolysis, which, when extended, stacks up lactate ions in the blood. At this point, the lactate shuttle system has to go into high gear to convert lactate back to ATP. Examples of lactate ladder workouts include the following:

❑ *Workout #1:* Run for 60 seconds at 800 meters effort, and then without stopping, cut down to a 3k pace for 90 seconds, before running for 120 seconds at a 5k pace. Finally, run easy for three minutes and then repeat. Begin with three sets and then work up to melt-down.

❑ *Workout #2:* Run for 60 seconds at 1500 meters pace, and then 90 seconds at a 5k pace, followed by 120 seconds at a 10k effort. Finally, run easy for three minutes and then repeat.

❑ *Workout #3:* Run at all out relaxed effort for 60 seconds and then easy for 120 seconds. Repeat until exhaustion sets in and you can no longer run completely relaxed.

CHAPTER 5
Training

Thousands of articles, books, and research papers have been written, purporting to tell runners what to run when training to race in endurance events. On the other hand, relatively little information exists on "how" to run. In reality, a number of runners cannot run fast when they need to during an endurance race, simply because they have not been taught how to run fast.

Coaches need to teach all their runners proper running mechanics before they develop poor running-form actions and bad habits. Overcoming poor running mechanics requires the abandonment of a runner's self-interpretation of running form, as well as a coach with a discerning eye for proper running form and a willingness to assist the runner to accept the prospect of learning new running skills. An excellent example of proper running form is that of Ethiopian Haile Gebrselassie. Runners should attempt to emulate his efficient, economical, and fast-stride rhythm to improve their own ability to run fast.

A number of the East African runners run as if they are running on hot coals. Training with a minimum of 96 turnovers per minute during their steady-state runs, they then increase their stride rate when picking up the pace. In many of their training sessions, they run as fast as possible for long periods, while staying relaxed.

Endurance running is often presented as a one-dimensional act, e.g., the development of the heart and circulatory system. While the cardiovascular system plays a very important role in any training scheme for training to race in distances of 800 meters to the marathon, the body's neuromuscular system and the mental aspects of running make training for endurance running a three-dimensional program. The central nervous system is in total control of all aspects of running.

Active running begins with the brain telling the feet to move. The message is sent to the spinal column and all of the neuromuscular components of the body, causing muscular contractions and relaxations that produce forward movement. Prolonged muscular contraction requires oxygen, in concert with aerobic glycolysis, to produce the energy that is required for doing the work of running. When oxygen and fuel burn, the heart responds by supplying oxygen-rich blood to the muscle fibers in the amount requested. This process is controlled by the brain. If a person wants to be a complete runner and train to race endurance events, they must develop all of the neuromuscular, cardiovascular, and mental potential that they have within their inherent makeup. No two individuals have exactly the same genetic potential.

Science has broken down genetic potentials into neuromuscular and cardiopulmonary variables. Anyone expecting to develop their potential to their optimal performance level must include all these variables in their training scheme, with all of the variables deployed concurrently in a progression of volume and intensity. Since running is initiated by the neural system, and the cardiopulmonary system is virtually a slave to the neural process, it is essential to begin each season with developing the neuromuscular variables that are fundamental to endurance running. Neural training teaches the muscular system to coordinate the contraction and relaxation of each fiber in a manner that produces the most power for running, as well as to work efficiently throughout the entire process of a race or workout.

There are three important aspects of neural training for runners. First, develop overall body strength and strengthen the muscles to do the work of running through dynamic movements that are specific to the act of running. Second, develop a running model that is as close to the overall running technique of a world-class athlete as possible. Third, develop a turnover and stride length that is most relevant to the velocity of the distance of the event to be raced, with a foot strike that is quick on and off the surface.

The neuromuscular aspects, which can easily be integrated into the warm-up and cool-down, are an integral part of skill work. In the beginning, the emphasis is on learning how to do the drills and activities correctly. This phase of the workout could initially take up to 45 minutes, and then is gradually reduced as runners become familiar with the drills.

The ultimate limitation on race performance for endurance events lies within the nervous system. The brain integrates sensory input from the muscles, tendons, and respiratory system during strenuous exercise. Regardless of how much cardiovascular power output that your training scheme could create, the essence of racing in endurance events is the power that is generated as each foot strikes the running surface.

The foot is a lever and does the work of running. The foot has genetically evolved into a practical tool for moving animals from one place to another. The human foot is composed of a heel bone with flexible appendages attached. It is constructed to help absorb the body's weight each time a step is taken and then becomes a lever to do the work of moving the body forward. The contour and stretch properties of the foot make it possible for a human to run at high velocities.

As a foot is brought into position under the runner's center of mass and makes contact just in front of the heel bone slightly to the outside, the arch and other appendages of the foot go into stretch, storing potential kinetic energy. As a runner's center of mass moves in front of the fulcrum of the foot, the weight shifts slightly inside (pronation), and slightly to the outside (supination).

As the toes dig into the running surface, the foot literally screws itself into the surface, which produces a clawing action that grabs the earth pushing it backwards, consequently sending the body forward. Other ligaments and muscles of the legs and buttocks also go on to stretch at touchdown, providing supporting elastic power to that of the foot lever. These coordinated stretching efforts provide a power level that extends from the buttocks down through the large toes.

An endurance runner must be able to maintain a relatively high velocity over the course of a race. This factor emphasizes the role of the neuromuscular characteristics related to voluntary and reflex neural-activation muscle force, flexibility, and running mechanics, as well as an inherent aerobics-related element. Collectively, they can differentiate well-trained endurance athletes, according to their racing performance. In order to develop the complete runner, instruction must be given in the skills of running mechanics and in running-specific muscle strengthening.

Some athletes establish a stride cycle that is too elongated with the slow on- and off-foot strike. As their training mileage builds in an effort to develop a higher $\dot{V}O_2max$, their central nervous system is being programmed to create neuromuscular patterns that are not conducive to fast racing.

In reality, the conventional theory that submaximal running velocities must be incorporated first to establish a base to gradually improve muscle strength, before including any speed, is a misconception. Mega miles run at submaximal velocities teaches the neuromuscular system to recruit mostly slow-twitch fibers and does not prepare the muscles for race-training velocities. Adding speed work later in the training scheme does not allow enough time to integrate the appropriate amount of speed training to become reactive in the neuromuscular system.

Because speed training that occurs later in the training scheme can lead to a heightened risk of injuries, speed work must begin with the very first practice of the season. While every runner can improve their basic speed, it takes hours of diligent practice, using drills and functional muscle-strengthening activities. Running fast intervals will improve an individual's race times by improving their ability to hold a pace that is closer to a specific percentage of their basic speed for a longer period. In other words, with proper training, a runner can eventually run a 10k at their current 5k race pace. Improving pure speed, however, can only come from conditioning the neuromuscular system to produce faster contractions that lend to more dynamic and forceful foot strikes.

Speed orientation begins by teaching athletes to learn how to run with gold-medal form. They need to learn to emulate, as closely as possible, the running action of the gold medal winners at the World Championships and Olympic Games. In other words, they need to maintain a tall, upright posture, with the head and shoulders directly above the hips. Runner should exhibit quick, but relaxed, arm action in a medium-length stride, with the fast turnover and quick foot strike. Their frontside mechanic should entail a knee-up, toe-up that allows for quick underneath drive of the foot. The foot strikes the surface as far back into the center of mass is possible, causing a midfoot touchdown.

When the foot pushes off the running surface, the heel is quickly driven directly under the buttock, forming a short lever, with the foot crossing the support leg slightly above the knee. This action prepares the foot to be in position for another quick and forceful foot strike. The muscles that cause this action are the quads, hamstrings, buttocks, and core. By performing functional strengthening activities, these muscles become strong and fatigue-resistant, which will not only allow the runner to hold the fast pace, but to answer any surges during the race and respond to the finishing speed of other athletes.

Running is accomplished by moving forward one step at a time, using a springy action made possible by the elastic springs in our feet and legs. Energy is stored during each foot strike and released at toe-off, making the act of running energy-efficient. To become an accomplished runner, an individual must move forward with a coordinated combination of stride length and stride frequency of the lower limbs, with balance and stabilization help from the upper limbs and core.

The neural system is in command of all muscular actions that are involved in running. An inability of the neural system to maintain balance limits capacity for optimum stride length, especially when running at medium-to-maximum running velocities, e.g., $\dot{V}O_2$max running velocities. Sensor input from the central nervous system will, in effect, regulate stride length and stride frequency.

During an endurance race, the body continues to struggle for balance and stability. The center of mass passes over the support limb. As such, the body must maintain dynamic equilibrium, e.g., a tall erect torso, with the head, shoulders, and hips in line directly over the collapsed support foot. As an endurance runner becomes more efficient through training, their running economy improves. Through running, the body develops its own combination of stride length and frequency in its effort to achieve a desired velocity.

Dr. Ralph Mann, silver medalist in the 400m hurdles at the 1972 Olympic Games and a pioneer in conducting research, has shown through high-speed, motion-analysis studies that too much time in the air and too much time on the ground hinder velocity movement. He has also found that reducing foot contract time by as little as 1/100th of a second produces marked improvement in races of any distance, mainly because reducing foot-strike time improves stride rate (turnover). Foot-strike time, turnover, and heel cycle determines race times. A lack of functional running strength to maintain a rhythmical stride length that is compatible with the desired turnover leads to overstriding and an inefficient use of energy.

Positioning the trunk to achieve balance, correct arm action, and proper foot strike are learned through performing running skill drills and engaging in functional strength activities. Improving maximal aerobic power is of the utmost importance in the development of an athlete's ability to race in an endurance event. Running alone, however, will not develop maximal neuromuscular power. *Coaches and athletes should understand that running is first a neural thing and that developing the neuromuscular system can no longer be ignored. They must come to the understanding that aerobic power and neuromuscular power have to be developed concurrently, not separately or singularly.*

The neural system creates muscular contractions. In order to run faster, scientific research shows that athletes must teach the nervous system to not only stimulate the muscles that generate greater force in a shorter period of time, but must also improve the manner in which the nervous system integrates muscular activity. Muscles that create propulsive force must be stimulated at just the right time, and muscles that might restrict movement must be relaxed at the proper moment. Muscles will not automatically do this themselves and must be coached to respond to the commands of the nervous system.

Running mile after mile at moderate velocities is not neural training. In fact, it is a detriment to fast running, because it does not promote the ability of the nervous system to generate high muscular force. As a result, it restricts basic genetic speed. Neural training features quick, forceful movements, and places a high premium on coordinating muscular activity in the most efficient manner possible. Quick, forceful contractions are desirable for endurance runners, if they expect to reach their optimal race performance.

Athletes cannot become a complete runner through running training alone. They have to supplement aerobic power development with dynamic warm-ups and circuit training that promotes functional leg strength and quick foot strikes. If coaches would allot just 30 percent of practice time to developing the neuromuscular aspects of running, they would be amazed at the improvement in race performance by their athletes. By exposing athletes to a concentrated program of perfecting their running skills and improving their strength in the muscles that do the work of running through functional strengthening activities, a more complete runner is produced.

The true measure of a nation's training scheme is how its athletes perform at a World Championship event. Over the past four decades, the United States has fallen woefully short of being productive at the elite level of world competition in endurance-racing events. Hundreds of thousands of youth and high school athletes participate in cross-country in this nation, with a relatively large percentage of them continuing on to compete in track endurance events, giving them year-round exposure to coaching.

Eventually, some of these athletes will compete at the college level, which provides the United States with a farm system unequaled by any other nation. Since this situation is a fact, wherein lays the fault of disappointing results in World Championship races? I believe one main reason for this problem is the coaching and training schemes in use at the entry-level to the sport and its continued use throughout the following 10 years of competing in endurance events.

Albert Einstein once said, "We cannot solve problems today by using the same kind of thinking we use to create them." At the present time, most coaches and athletes are satisfied with the results of the training scheme that addresses cardiovascular enhancement almost exclusively. American coaches and athletes are locked into a training tradition that entails the following sequence: first, they develop $\dot{V}O_2max$, using mileage quotas; then, they use tempo runs to improve lactate threshold; third, for strength, they add intervals, hills and weightlifting; and finally, they implement some type of speed work during the latter part of the season. Most of these training programs are based on and evaluated by how much mileage is run each week, an approach that focuses solely on developing the cardiovascular system. The neuromuscular power that develops occurs without help from the functional muscle strengthening activities, simply because they are not employed.

The primary problem with this traditional training scheme is that it does not produce a complete runner. A complete runner is an athlete who can hold the race pace, answer surges, and respond to the finishing kick of other athletes. Traditional coaching methods have produced many runners who are proficient at holding race pace, yet fail when it comes to answering surges and/or being able to respond to the finishing speed of other runners. More often than not, traditionally trained runners cannot run fast enough during the critical stages of a race, because no one ever taught them how to run fast.

The current training manual published by USA Track and Field Coaches Education Committee continues to concentrate on instructing coaches to use traditional training methods for their athletes and virtually ignores the neuromuscular aspects of running. There are three essential aspects of neural training. First, to develop the overall body strength, specifically those muscles that do the work of running through dynamic movements that are specific to the act of running. Second, to develop a running model that is as close to the overall technique of world champion athletes as possible, which entails having a turnover and stride length that is very relevant to the velocity of the distance raced. The runner's foot strike, which is quick on and off the surface, is accomplished through proper frontside and backside mechanics. Third, to improve eccentric functional muscle strength in the muscles that provide stretch energy for running power and condition those muscles to resist fatigue throughout the entire endurance race.

Why doesn't the traditional method of coaching endurance athletes produce more medals at the Olympics and World Championships? I believe the basic reason for this dilemma is that many of the methods developing the various psychological variables of endurance are based more on "hand-me-down" information or myths, rather than proven scientific research.

The first myth is that an athlete must achieve an aerobic base before developing other physiological variables, and the best way to do this is through running mega miles at a moderate pace. There are some glaring misconceptions in this theory of training. Because running is primarily a neural issue, running a lot of miles at a moderate pace is not neural training, because it does not promote the ability of the nervous system to generate high muscular force. Instead, it produces a slow turnover and foot strike that retards the genetic qualities that generate speed for racing. Moreover, running lots of miles at slow paces will eventually enhance $\dot{V}O_2max$ in beginning runners, but not in well-trained runners. In actuality, $\dot{V}O_2max$ is enhanced with an upswing in training intensity and a reduction in mileage.

In reality, if a good cardiovascular foundation is established without a well-developed nervous system, an athlete cannot reach their optimal potential and racing. All of the physiological variables, both neural and cardiovascular, must be developed concurrently, as opposed to one before another.

Another myth is that periodization of training, which simply refers to changes in volume, intensity, and frequency of training over time, follows a linear progression. In such a technique, athletes generally either build up their total volume of training in a linear way or gradually decrease the volume, while steadily increasing their training intensity. This type of training is broken into macrocycles, mesocycles, and microcycles.

The underlying premise of this theory is that athletes need to build up some level of general strength and endurance before attempting high-intensity training. In reality, there is no scientific basis for this premise, given that athletes are capable of carrying out reasonable amounts of intense training from the start of the training season. It takes immense effort to compete in endurance events and for a runner to be successful, intense training is necessary.

A base for hard efforts can begin the first day of practice using drills and functional muscle strengthening. In contrast to linear periodization is undulating periodization. The undulating periodization plan allows for alternating intensity and volume. For example, an athlete might move from high-volume, low-intensity work to low-volume, high-intensity training within the same week.

In general, with undulating periodization, the phases of training tend to be much shorter in time. As such, frequent changes in training stimuli are very conducive to gains in fitness. When these stimuli are presented together in close time-period proximity, the neuromuscular system can adapt unusually quickly and develop an enhanced ability to respond with great force and quickness. Conversely, speed work early in the week, tempo runs in midweek, and a long run on weekends are not a good building block in a training month and not a solid foundation for six-month prep for major event.

If coaches base an athlete's periodization on systematically enhancing strength and speed at the same time, they can take advantage of the stress and adaptation phenomenon and consistently improve the runner's level of fitness. As noted previously, all physiological variables can gain strength over a period of 21 days. These variables then tend to level off for seven days. Accordingly, a training period of 28 days allows 21 days for an upswing in fitness, with the following seven days to recover, before again pushing the intensity of volume to the next level.

During a competitive season, endurance athletes perform best during an upswing in their fitness. With this factor in mind, coaches can fit their training efforts to coincide with important races, if entry-level endurance athletes are exposed to a training scheme that promotes both cardiovascular capacity and neuromuscular power concurrently during their first 10 years of development. Furthermore, those individuals who eventually reach elite status will be better able to cope with world-class competition.

A third myth is that an athlete's $\dot{V}O_2$ is the best predictor of racing potential. Traditional training emphasizes the development of an athlete's maximal oxygen uptake as the key to racing in endurance events. This theory purports that the more oxygen can be consumed and utilized by working muscles, the greater potential for racing. In reality, scientific studies show that $\dot{V}O_2$ rating is not the greatest predictor of racing potential.

Two athletes with the same $\dot{V}O_2$ do not usually finish a race together, because one of them will have a better running economy, a better the $\dot{V}O_2max$, a lower lactate threshold running velocity (LTRV), or better speed. Running economy, which is the oxygen uptake needed to run at a specific velocity, is enhanced when a lower percentage of energy is expended. The $\dot{vV}O_2max$ is the lowest running velocity at which $\dot{V}O_2max$ occurs. LTRV is the running velocity at which lactate threshold is reached.

A more valid predictor of endurance racing potential is the run-to-exhaustion test. This test is designed to determine how long a person can run at a specific velocity, before becoming exhausted to point of having to stop due to the complete breakdown of the working muscles. A training program whose major goal is to increase the supply of oxygen for ongoing glycolysis is ignoring the basis for continuing the production of energy.

Glycolysis is not the most important physiological variable in running, but rather the production of lactic acid (lactate), which is a byproduct of glycolysis. While glycolysis will continue to produce energy, when lactate accumulates in the blood faster than being converted back to energy, the muscles cannot continue to function at a high level. Too much lactate acid in the blood stream will cause pain. Subsequently, the brain will tell the muscles to shut down or be destroyed. It behooves coaches to insert workouts from the start of the season that teach muscles to shuttle lactate ions into the mitochondria, where, through the Krebs cycle, they are changed to ATP, the body's basic source of energy.

In order to take full advantage of the energy produced by glycolysis, it is necessary to develop an efficient lactate conversion system. No aerobic energy is produced until some anaerobic energy is produced. By exposing the endurance athlete to high lactate-producing workouts early in the training scheme, the muscles will quickly learn how to allow glycolysis to continue to produce energy for running.

The key to running faster for long periods of time is to recycle lactate produced through glycolysis and change it back to ATP for energy production. In order to run fast for a specific distance, an athlete must not only recruit fast-twitch muscle fibers and maintain the production of fuel for energy, it must also accomplish both objectives with a high degree of efficiency. To run fast, the muscles have to be trained to work fast. To run with high intensity for an extended period of time, it is necessary to develop the physiological variables that improve the ability of the body to generate energy as the work continues.

Training athletes to race in endurance events is simply a matter of training muscle fibers so they become stronger and more efficient. All of the muscles that do the work of running, along with all the organs involved, are composed of specific types of muscle cells. The heart, lungs, capillaries, and skeletal muscles are composed of muscle cells that respond to training.

As noted previously, all muscle cells respond to the stress and adaptation phenomenon. Muscle cells combine into fibers, which provide the tensile strength for running. When muscles are stressed beyond their present capacity, a signal is sent to the brain that is interpreted as pain. Not liking pain, the muscles adapt to this level of stress and become stronger in the process. Coaches can use this phenomenon of stress and adaptation of muscle cells to plan their training schemes. Coaches can periodize training, based on strength and speed, and logically address all of the relevant physiological variables in a sequence that would develop the complete runner.

The traditional schemes of training employed by most coaches in the United States do not produce complete runners. A complete runner is an athlete who can respond to surges and cover the finishing kicks of other runners. If we are to gain prominence in the world of endurance running, changes to our philosophy of training need to be made. This training program should begin with our youth and should be consistent throughout the runner's collegiate career. Coaches, who are setting the standard for training, need to reevaluate the overall scheme for training endurance runners. The latest scientific research, along with a review and consideration of what successful coaches in other countries are doing, should be incorporated into their training schemes.

Running is initiated and controlled by the brain and the neural capacities of the muscular system. Actions of the heart, lungs, and circulatory system remain in status quo until triggered by the neuromuscular system. The brain initiates a chain reaction of neural simulation that tells the muscular system how quickly and forcefully to contract, when to relax, and again when to initiate the act of running at the intensity and duration needed.

In reality, the nervous system of the athlete must be taught to coordinate contraction and relaxation during the stride cycle and creative foot strike that is quick on and off the surface. The foot then quickly and efficiently returns to a point that is as close to being under the center of mass is possible. An athlete who wants to run fast for long periods must teach their muscles to become strong, as well as condition the tissue strips along the bottom of the foot, the Achilles tendon and associated muscles, the prevalent muscles and tendons around the knee, and the key muscles and tendons of the hips.

All these tissues are stretched as the foot strikes the ground, increasing the potential energy of the leg muscles. At toe-off, the stretched tissues snap back, returning about 90 percent of their stored energy, with 10 percent being lost as heat.

If the feet, legs, and hips were not able to store the energy, the working muscles would have to increase their work output and energy expenditure by approximately 50 percent. The key parts of the body for storing energy are the feet and the Achilles tendons. As the center of a runner's mass moves ahead of the fulcrum of the foot, these two stressed body parts snap back to their original position. The uncoiling of these two springs provide the direct force for forward movement, while the buttocks and hamstring muscles continue to push downward, until the toes leave the surface. These two muscles provide continuing impetus for forward movement, while positioning the legs to resume the stride cycle.

A traditional training program concentrates almost entirely on producing cardiopulmonary power, with little or no attention given to the production of neuromuscular power. Most coaches and athletes are aware of the neural aspects of running, but either do not understand how to facilitate these aspects or choose not to include them in their training scheme. In that regard, the primary purpose of this book is to explain them fully and to provide training exercises to implement them. In reality, it is necessary for coaches and athletes to recognize and capitalize on the fact the running begins with the central nervous system, by initiating pertinent muscle fiber contractions and relaxations within the neuromuscular system. As such, training schemes need to include neuromuscular-enhancement activities, beginning with youth and high school programs and continuing on to collegiate competition.

The brain initiates running and the actions of a runner's neuromuscular system, which stimulates contraction. The heart and lungs remain at the resting rate until stimulated by a demand for oxygen, which is created through muscle contractions. The intensity and duration of contractions determine how fast and how long the heart muscle must accelerate its rate of work in order to supply the amount of oxygen demanded.

The strength of the heart muscle is limited by the extent to which the duration and intensity of muscle contraction occurs. The duration and intensity of muscle contraction is limited by the strength and power of the muscles that do the work of running. In reality, the heart, lungs, and circulatory system are dependent upon the strength and power of the working muscles for their strength and functionality.

Continuous muscle contraction requires more oxygen. The need of additional oxygen alerts the brain, which signals the heart to beat faster and harder in order to supply this new demand. In the simplest of terms, running is first a neural thing and cardiopulmonary a second thing. To put it another way, when the heart and circulatory systems deliver oxygen and nutrients to the neuromuscular system, it is because the central nervous system signals them to do so. The brain is the boss.

Functionally strengthening the muscles that do the work of running, along with performing running-skill drills, produces an increase in speed and a more economical use of energy. With a solid foundation of neuromuscular training, coordinated with multi-tiered velocities of running, every athlete will progressively raise their fitness level.

CHAPTER 6 ━━━━━━━━━━
Competition Training

A review of the endurance distance race results at the World Championships and Olympic Games shows the athletes with the best closing speed winning the medals. Athletes displaying quicker feet and a faster turnover usually finish at the top. Traditional schemes of training do not produce a complete runner. A complete runner is an athlete who can respond to surges and cover the finishing kicks of the other runners. Traditional training programs concentrate almost entirely on producing cardiopulmonary power, with little or no attention being given to the production of neuromuscular power.

Most coaches and athletes are aware of the neural aspects of running, but either do not understand how to facilitate these aspects, or choose not to include them in their training scheme. If coaches include neuromuscular enhancement activities in youth and high school programs and continue to use them during the individual's years of collegiate competition, America's elite athletes will be able to compete against the best runners in the world. Coaches and athletes need to recognize and capitalize on the fact that running begins with the central nervous system and is carried out by muscle fiber contractions and relaxation within the neuromuscular system.

Continued muscle contraction requires more oxygen. The need for oxygen alerts the brain, which signals the heart to beat faster in order to supply this new demand. In the simplest terms, running is thus a neural thing first and a cardiopulmonary thing second. To put it another way, when the heart and circulatory systems deliver oxygen and nutrients to the neuromuscular system, it is because the brain tells them to do so.

Research has established the fact that the functional strengthening of muscles that do the work of running, along with performing running-skill drills, will produce increased speed and more economical use of energy. The key to running fast is to be able to create a foot strike that can produce a backward thrust equal to or greater than the center of gravity is moving forward. Constant attention must be given to developing running strength and fatigue-resistant muscle training throughout an athlete's entire racing career.

When running, every time the foot touches down, energy is absorbed and stored by the muscles and tendons of the legs. During each foot strike, the body is slowed and lowered and then raised and sped up at toe-off. The absorbed energy provides the power to lift and accelerate the body forward until the collision between the other foot and the ground. During the time in the air, no energy is being used, since the energy is already stored during the foot strike. Upon impact, however, muscles and tendons recoil like rubber bands, providing the power for forward propulsion.

During the support phase of running, some muscles must actively expend energy to provide the force necessary to support the body, while keeping it upright, hopefully in an efficient position for running. The supporting role of muscles, while the foot is on the ground, is the result of isometric muscle actions that take place without any shortening of the muscle. The stability of the upper body is the result of the isometric action of the abdominal and lower back muscles.

The calf muscle, in its role of absorbing the force of landing, helps accelerate the foot downward to the ground, as the ankle extends, using very little energy through contraction. Runners with better muscle contractibility are able to produce higher rates of oxygen consumption and can handle correspondingly higher workloads than those athletes with lesser muscle contractility. This factor is especially important during intense workouts.

The runner who can work at a higher percentage of $\dot{V}O_2max$ pace and $\dot{V}O_2max$ should be able to produce greater adaptations in the key variables of endurance physiology, than those athletes who work at lower percentages. The higher muscle contractibility potential is an aerobic attribute, which determines the power output of the muscles and is an important ingredient in determining aerobic adaptations. Runners whose muscles are capable of fast force production, with rapid, well-coordinated explosive contractions, have a decided advantage in endurance events.

Exercise physiologists have shown that 5k velocity is inversely proportionate to foot strike time. The best 5k runners will be those individuals with the most powerful neuromuscular characteristics that can produce explosive foot strikes. There are six very important factors relating to endurance distance runners. First, a reduction in foot strike time of 1/300th of a second will reduce a 5k meter race time by up to 10 seconds, as long as the stride length is not reduced. Second, a reduction of foot strike time by l/100th of a second can lower 5k times by up to 30 seconds. Third, improving foot strike time will result in faster 5k times, once $\dot{V}O_2max$ pace and LT have reached a high level. Fourth, a stride rate and length are also important variables in determining 5k potential. The faster the stride rate, the faster the 5k time, assuming the stride length isn't reduced. Fifth, the fastest 5k runners also have the fastest 20 meters, 50 meters, and 300 meter times. Finally, sixth, speed is the most important ingredient in determining the runner's potential to race at any distance.

Neuromuscular strengthening is the key to improving and should include optimizing coordination of contractions and relaxation of muscles, so that the least amount of force production is needed to stabilize unnecessary movements, such an attribute allows all of the muscle energy to be channeled into propulsion. This strengthening involves a systematic process of proprioceptive training, which encompasses conditioning the neuromuscular system to coordinate all sensory activity to produce better overall strength, coordination, and muscular balance during athletic performance.

A proprioceptor is one of a variety of sensory-end organs, such as are found in the muscle spindle and Golgi's tendon organ, as well as in muscles, tendons, and joint capsules that are sensitive to the stimuli originating by the movement of the body or its parts. The body uses up energy supporting itself in the upright position, while keeping the ankles and lower legs from collapsing. A runner can save energy if they have sufficient upper-body strength to keep the head balanced to prevent it from moving forward or backward and from side-to-side.

Coaches and athletes do not have to understand all of the intricacies of the central nervous system in order to implement neuromuscular training. As a coach or an athlete, all they need to do is to incorporate these dynamic activities into circuit workouts and into the warm-up and cooldown phases of the workouts. So, instead of doing the traditional jogging and static stretching to warm-up and cool-down, they should require their athletes to perform dynamic movements that promote flexibility, strength, and running rhythm.

Many of these dynamic activities mimic the act of running and are ballistic in nature, but some are designed to strengthen the upper body as well. A strong upper-body, along with strong core muscles, helps maintain a tall, upright posture and eliminate unnecessary movements during the act of running, thereby enhancing running economy. Performing running-skill drills will improve the dynamic equilibrium and coordination between turnovers and stride length, with an emphasis on quick on-and-off foot strikes, which will develop speed and running efficiency.

The overall ability of the body to supply oxygen to all the muscle cells is known as $\dot{V}O_2max$ or maximal oxygen uptake. Preparing to race in endurance events is simply a matter of training the muscle cells that compose the organs and skeletal muscles involved in the exercise to perform specific actions. In reality, all muscle cells respond to the phenomenon of stress and adaptation.

The heart is dominate in the chain of muscles that make up the human body, since all muscle cells rely on oxygen-rich blood for their substance and functions. The heart, which has the highest $\dot{V}O_2max$ of any of the muscles, has no limitation on the extent to which it can be stressed. The more the muscles that do the work of running are stressed, the stronger the heart muscle becomes, which, in turn, allows the muscles to do more work.

$\dot{V}O_2max$ is referred to as *aerobic power*, because it is a measure of the rate at which oxygen is consumed. It is especially important for the middle distance events, from 800 meters to 3,000 meters, which are run at close to 100 percent of $\dot{V}O_2max$. The two key components for training to race in endurance events is the development of cardiovascular and neuromuscular strength.

The cardiovascular system produces the fuel for muscle contraction. Cardio power is determined by the stroke volume of the heart, the extent of capillary growth, and the number and size of mitochondria within each muscle cell. Stroke volume is the amount of blood pumped by the left ventricle of the heart per beat and is determined by the return of blood back to the heart through venous circulation (venous return). The larger the left ventricle is, the more blood it can hold and, subsequently, the more it can pump. The amounts of oxygen that can be extracted and used by the muscles are dependent on mitochondrial and capillary volumes. The more capillaries that perfuse the muscle fibers, the shorter the diffusion distance for oxygen from the capillaries to the mitochondria, which are the microscopic "energy powerhouses" that contain the enzymes involved in aerobic metabolism.

The number of enzymes is important because enzymes control 80 to 85 percent of $\dot{V}O_2max$. If the heart is unable to send all the oxygenated blood to the muscles that they demand during exertion, the heart is the limiting factor for preventing $\dot{V}O_2max$ from reaching its optimal level. If muscles are unable to use all of the oxygen sent to them, then the muscles are a problem.

The process for producing fuel for cardio power is called glycolysis. Glycolysis is the process by which oxygen mixes with the fuel from what individuals eat to produce the energy that is required in a bout of exercise. In essence, glycolysis, which is essential to cardio power development, provides fuel for continuous work. One of the products that is produced as glucose (blood sugar) is broken down is lactate.

Lactate is recycled through the mitochondria in each cell back to ATP, which is the essential energy component for running. ATP must be constantly reproduced, since muscular contractions deplete it rapidly. When lactate is produced faster than it can be converted back to ATP, the muscles become overacidic (acidosis) and begin to shut down.

The running velocity at which lactate levels begin to pile up in your blood stream faster than it can be converted back to energy is referred to as an individual's lactate threshold (LT). The improvement of LT running velocity (LTRV) is absolutely essential to running fast for long periods of time. Not only does lactate conversion provide a great muscle fuel, LTRV is also a good barometer of muscle function during exercise. If lactate floods the muscles at a moderate running pace, the muscles are not adequately prepared for high quality efforts. If lactate does not pool in the blood stream until fast paces are reached, the muscles are doing an excellent job of using lactate as fuel.

When a person's cardio and neural systems are exposed to specific running velocities, both systems will adapt to race at those specific paces. The more athletes train at a specific velocity, the more efficient they become at that velocity. In order to produce energy for continuous running, the body must be taught to recycle lactate quickly and efficiently. This factor gives workouts that teach this phenomenon a high priority when planning a training scheme to race in endurance events. Accordingly, it is necessary to insert workouts that produce excessive lactate early into an athlete's training scheme so the muscles can learn quickly how to convert lactate back to useable energy. Training for the development of all physiological variables concurrently at multi-tiered velocities will ensure a high level of fitness and a more complete runner.

The human mind monitors carbohydrate oxidation during exercise. Five kilos per hour (19:00/mile) is the universal walking speed, a rate which is reasonably comfortable. Furthermore, the brain is content with the perceived effort at this speed, because carbohydrate burning is minimal at this pace.

Walking at this velocity is an important threshold, because a person automatically adjusts their gait to minimize energy cost. If a person wants to go faster than two meters per second, they will run, because the act of running is more oxygen-economical than walking at such a pace. When the velocity of running is increased, the oxidation process produces lactate in sufficient quantities to accumulate rapidly in the blood stream.

This phenomenon is not related to a lack of oxygen, but rather to a shuttle system, which converts lactate back to glycogen. This shuttle system exists in the walls of muscle cells, where mitochondria convert lactate back to energy. A practical comparison of the lactate balance phenomenon is explained by Jason R. Karp, in his article on lactate threshold published in *Track Coach* (Fall 2007). "Think of a bucket with a hole in it that sits out in the rain. When it is raining lightly, the bucket empties through the hole. On the other hand, when it is pouring, water fills the bucket faster than it empties, and water accumulates in the bucket. If the rainfall is heavy enough, the bucket will overflow. When the rainfall equals the amount of water exiting the hole, the water level remains at a constant level."

When such a homeostasis is reached in the muscle cell, a lactate threshold is established. Lactate threshold is the balance between purely aerobic exercise that includes significant oxygen, and independent anaerobic metabolism. Lactate threshold is also the acidosis threshold, since it is the acidosis that is of interest rather than lactate. The accumulation of lactate is only a reflection of the state of acidosis.

The running velocity at which LT is reached is a great predictor of a person's potential to race in endurance events. When an individual is running at a speed that is faster than LTRV, hydrogen ions accumulate in the body at a rapid rate, producing an intracellular acidity that upsets the PH balance. A buildup of hydrogen ions plays havoc with energy-producing enzyme activity and disrupts the action of some of the contractible proteins.

When this situation occurs, a runner's buffering process must be improved. The body produces its own buffering compounds, which play a significant role in the buffering process. Training at intense velocities can definitely improve the buffering process and help the intramuscular proteins gather these ions and transport them out of the muscle cells. Highly trained soccer players, sprinters, and rowers have excellent buffering capacities, whereas marathoners tend to have relatively lower buffering velocity.

The production of neuromuscular power is equally important to racing as is cardio power. Neuromuscular power is developed through functional muscle strengthening, speed and economical mechanics. Having a super strong heart is just one race-related factor involved in a runner's optimal ability. If a runner cannot create the force necessary to run fast for long periods of time and then produce even more force during critical stages of a race, the runner won't be as good as they could possibly be. Neuromuscular training must be given adequate attention in the training scheme in order for runners to race at their optimum ability in endurance events. This step can be accomplished through the use of dynamic and functional activities performed during warm-ups and cool-downs, along with circuit training. Teaching running skills is a continuous task for the coach throughout every practice session.

A Training Scheme to Prepare an Athlete to Compete in Endurance Races

The training plan detailed in this section is based on the insights and information gained during over 60 years of coaching experience, as well as being corroborated by the latest scientific research. The principles of the training plan can be modified to prepare youth, high school, collegiate, elite, and masters endurance athletes to race in any event from the 800 meters to the marathon. All endurance runners, regardless of age or ability, need to maximize training that enhances $\dot{V}O_2max$, $v\dot{V}O_2max$, lactate threshold running velocity (LTRV), running efficiency, power, speed, and functional muscle strength.

Developing an impressive $\dot{V}O_2max$ is not enough to become a complete runner because an athlete must also be able to answer surges and respond to the finishing speed of other athletes. All the kinetics of running is controlled by the neuromuscular system, thereby determining the intensities and duration of a muscle contraction, as well as coordinating the contraction and relaxation of each fiber. The mechanics of running, which play a critical role in races of any distance, must be given equal training time. Efficient and powerful running is not only a mechanical issue, but also involves functional muscle strengthening to reduce fatigue and provide ongoing power.

Research indicates that a person's basic speed is the most important physiological variable in determining a person's potential to race at any distance. Research also shows that up to 20 percent of the lactic acid produced from glycolysis during running can be changed back to useful energy by properly conditioned endurance athletes. Teaching the muscles to recycle lactic acid back to useable energy demands that the issue be accorded a prominent position in any training scheme for endurance runners, because the faster pace that they can hold, while not overdosing on lactate buildup, the better their ability to race. This factor is known as an individual's lactate threshold running velocity (LTRV). A runner's LTRV is a great predictor of their ability to race at any event from 800 meters through the marathon.

A training scheme should build a base for all of the variables necessary for preparing athletes to race in endurance events. Such a scheme should address the following factors:

❑ #1: Develop Gold Medal Running Form

The first objective of the training scheme is to form a base for fast and efficient running and for improving a runner's 400-meter speed. Gold medal winners in the Olympic and World Championships, who all run with power and efficiency, are excellent role models.

❑ #2: Functional Strengthen the Muscles That Perform the Work of Running

In order to run with power and efficiency, an athlete must develop strong and fatigue-resistant working muscles. This objective is best accomplished by performing resistance work, while mimicking the act of running, along with some core and upper-body strengthening.

❑ #3: Improve Basic Speed

Athletes learn to run fast-relaxed for the longest possible time. Running fast-relaxed requires compete relaxation of the upper body and arms. An endurance runner's basic speed is their 400-meters time.

❑ #4: Improve the Muscular System's Ability to Recycle Lactic Acid Back to Useable Energy

A continuous flow of oxygen for glycolysis is fundamental for endurance running. It is the by-product of glycolysis, lactic acid, which when recycled back to ATP, provides energy for continuous running. Up to 20 percent of the lactic acid produced while running can be recycled to useful energy. Training the muscular system to recycle lactate back to ATP is essential and must be initiated at the very beginning of a training season.

❑ #5: Develop $\dot{V}O_2$max Functionally and Efficiently

While developing $\dot{V}O_2$max through a mileage quota of sub-maximal running velocities will improve a beginner's oxygen uptake over a period of time, it will do little to improve a seasoned runner's ability to supply oxygen to their circulatory system. Seasoned runners can best improve their $\dot{V}O_2$max through running at $v\dot{V}O_2$max velocity or faster. $v\dot{V}O_2$max is the running speed at which $\dot{V}O_2$max occurs. Employing quality running paces is the key to improving $\dot{V}O_2$max. Running sub-maximal paces to improve $\dot{V}O_2$max is not only inefficient, it also impedes basic speed by establishing a slow turnover and slow on-and-off foot strike.

❑ #6: Prepare to Race

The best preparation for racing is to take full advantage of the aforementioned sequence of training. To a degree, an athlete's fitness level determines the ability to race. In that regard, if individuals schedule their racing to coincide with an upswing in their fitness level, they give themselves the best chance to race well. Fitness levels tend to escalate over a 21-day cycle, and then level off for seven days before continuing again on an upswing. An endurance runner's fitness level can be determined either by their performance on a six-minute run for distance or from their race performance.

The next step in preparing to race is to establish the basic speed for the runner. Knowing an individual's 400 meters speed can be valuable in determining training and racing goals. How fast can a person run the 100 meters in a race? Is the athlete able to finish strong over the last 200 to 300 meters? Should the runner draft and then accelerate to improve their position? Is the runner able to build up speed over the last 600 meters and finish strong? These are some of the questions that coaches and athletes should ask themselves when determining race strategy and then try to answer them by incorporating a variety of different tactics in low-key races. A runner needs to learn which strategy works best for them and then get as much information as possible on other competitors in order to evaluate their strengths and weaknesses. Finally, runners need to trust their fitness level and then race to the limit.

Gold medal winners exhibit similar mechanical characteristics when they race. Their form features a tall, upright torso with the head and shoulders directly over the hips, which are rotated slightly forward. The arms are held loosely from the shoulders at a 90-degree angle. Their elbows are kept close to the rib cage, as the arms move forward and back, stopping at the midline of the chest and again at the backside of the hips, while they're moving backward. All the muscles of the shoulders and lower arms should be completely relaxed.

Ideally, a side view of the runner will show an explosive toe-off, with the thigh driving forward and upward. When the knee reaches the most forward position, the foot is vigorously snapped downward and back, causing it to strike the running surface as far back under the center of mass as possible, while making first contact on the flexible part of the foot. At toe-off, the foot moves upward, as the calf muscles collapse against the hamstring. This action creates a short lever for a quick return of the foot. The recovery foot crosses the support leg just above the knee.

The placement of the foot is extremely important, since it is the lever that provides the power to propel the body forward. The power leg is flexed as it pushes backward. It then becomes the recovery leg as it is driven forward at full flexion, with the ankle poised higher than the knee. In order to run fast, the athlete must maximize the leg recovery and touchdown rotation speed. Of all the upper-leg action, upper-leg speed at touchdown is the most critical, since it affects both the amount of forward braking and the amount of ground-contact time. The athlete must minimize the lower leg angle during both the recovery and as the ankle crosses over the support leg to run fast.

The production of forward movement is the key to fast running. It should be noted, however, the horizontal force is not the critical factor in making this happen. Once the runner has reached top speed, it is the vertical force that plays the critical role. Due to the presence of gravity, running action consists of a series of ground and air phases. To continue to run at a high velocity, the athlete must increase the vertical velocity at a point where the foot leaves the running surface. Then, during the air phase, gravitational pull rapidly reverses the runner's upward velocity, and as touchdown once again occurs, the athlete's vertical velocity has been altered. The maximum horizontal velocity that a runner can produce is dependent upon the amount of vertical force that can be applied (Figure 6-1). As such, the two most critical phases of fast running are the touchdown speed and the ankle crossover speed (Figure 6-2).

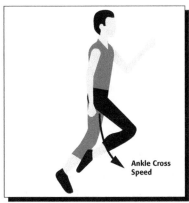

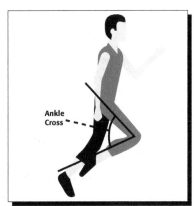

Figure 6-1   Figure 6-2

As noted previously, a runner's basic speed is the single most important physiological variable that determines the runner's ability to race at any distance. If an athlete is able to improve their basic speed, they will also enhance their speed in various race distances upwards, since races are always run at a percentage of a person's maximal running velocity. Runners can improve their basic speed by increasing stride rate or length without sacrificing the other. Stride length is a function of how much force the leg and foot can apply to the running surface. Running mechanics play a vital role in force production, since stride length is directly a result of how far back under the center of mass the foot touches down and how fast it is moving in a backward direction at contact. Overall, the force production must be well-coordinated. Functional strength exercises help coordinate the leg and foot action required for faster running.

Gains in strength and efficiency will also improve a runner's overall performance. Functional muscle strengthening is mostly carried out on one leg at a time, with full-body weight borne by that leg. When an athlete is exerting increased force, a large percentage of muscle strength stabilizes the leg at touchdown. The strengthening exercises should mimic the act of running as much as possible.

The three basic exercises used to stabilize and strengthen are high bench step-ups, feet-up squats and one-half squats, and vertical hops. A fourth exercise, box hops, uses both legs but involves eccentric muscle contraction. Muscular action utilized in running is mostly eccentric. As an individual's level of strength progresses, the athlete can add either additional weights or more sets (or both). Bounding, one-leg hops, and hill running are great functional strength building exercises. Strengthening the quads, buttocks, and hamstring muscles is absolutely a must if a runner is to hold a fast pace for extended periods of time.

Forming a foundation for running and racing with running skills, functional leg strength, and speed development provides the athlete with the opportunity to run efficiently for long periods of time. Specific competition speeds need to be completed at the lowest fraction of maximal energy cost or maximum aerobic capacity. As an individual runs, the easier an effort feels, the more room the athlete has to improve their competitive velocity. For instance, if a six-minute per mile running velocity is 99 percent of a person's $\dot{V}O_2max$, there is little possibility for that athlete to create more energy aerobically. On the other hand, if the individual can run a six-minute pace at only 92 percent of their maximum oxygen uptake, they have more potential to improve their racing velocity.

A person's ability to consume oxygen through physical exertion is represented by the measure $\dot{V}O_2max$. The more oxygen that a person can breathe in and send to the muscles throughout the blood stream, the greater the measure of $\dot{V}O_2max$. Even though $\dot{V}O_2max$ sets the parameter for aerobic power, it is not the best indicator of a runner's potential to perform in endurance races.

As noted previously, two athletes with the same $\dot{V}O_2max$ rating will probably perform quite differently in an endurance race. The one with better running economy or basic speed will win the race. The running velocity at which maximal aerobic velocity is attained, however, is a great predictor of racing potential. This running velocity is represented by the symbol $v\dot{V}O_2max$ and reveals both the magnitude of an individual's aerobic capabilities for running and the efficiency with which that person moves when running at very high speeds.

When an athlete runs, no aerobic energy can be created until some anaerobic energy is produced. When muscles break down food to ATP through the process of glycolysis, lactic acid (lactate) is a by-product of the burning of oxygen. The running velocity at which lactate levels begin to pile up in an individual's blood stream faster than it can be converted to energy is referred to as a person's lactate threshold (LT).

The improvement of LT running velocity (LTRV) is absolutely essential to running fast for long periods of time. Lactate conversion provides a great muscle fuel and LTRV is a barometer of muscle functioning during exercise. If lactate floods a runner's muscles at a moderate running speed, the individual's muscles are not adequately prepared for high quality efforts. If lactate does not pool in the blood stream until high speeds are reached, the muscles are doing an excellent job of using lactate as fuel.

When a person's cardio and neural systems are exposed to specific running velocities, both systems will adapt to racing at those specific paces. The more an athlete trains at a specific velocity, the more efficient they become at that velocity.

Training at multi-tiered velocities not only will help a person become a more complete runner, it will also ensure a high level of fitness. A training scheme must allow for the development of all physiological variables concurrently and not be restricted by a set time period for each one.

All of the drills and running-specific activities are designed to put the foot lever into a power position. The key parts of the leg lever are the arch of the foot and the Achilles tendon. Each time the foot strikes the ground, energy is stored as elastic strain energy. The upper and lower legs are composed of key springs in the form of connective tissue strips that run along the sole of the foot, the Achilles tendon, and the associated muscles, such as the calf and anterior tibialis.

Other prevalent muscles and tendons around the knee and hips are also stretched for elastic strain potential. All of these structures are stretched as the foot makes contact with the running surface, increasing the potential energy of the legs. At toe-off, these strained muscles and tendons return about 90 percent of the work required to stretch them. There is about a 10 percent heat loss in the total action.

If the tendons and muscles of the legs were not able to store energy during impact, the working muscles would have to increase their workload and energy expenditure by about 50 percent. The importance of strengthening these working muscles and tendons and teaching the neuromuscular system to produce correct running actions receives a great deal of attention, especially in the beginning of a competitive season, but are never neglected totally during the season.

Regardless of a person's age, whether it is 40, 50, 60, or even 70 plus, it does not mean that an individual cannot run fast. While aging does have an effect on stride length and running power, runners can conserve both for longer periods of time than a person might otherwise think. In fact, it is the disuse of the muscles that are specific to running that erodes performance more so than the aging process.

If the runner can develop a turnover of 96 (192 steps) per minute, there is little decline in stride rate, even at 50 years of age. Basically, runners slow with age because of a loss of power, functional leg strength, and range of motion that causes stride length to shorten. Mostly, a runner's ability declines with age, because their neuromuscular system has not been stimulated properly to maintain muscle consistency.

Humans begin to lose muscle strength and $\dot{V}O_2max$ after age 40; the losses can be slowed, however, through activities that stimulate the neuromuscular system to produce quicker and more forceful actions. Engaging in running-skill drills, functional muscle strengthening, and speed-enhancing activities will definitely slow the process of aging, as its affects racing in endurance events. All of the cells that comprise the organs and muscles that are involved in the physiology of running are muscle cells. When muscles contract to cause movement, an athlete's heart rate increases in its effort to send oxygen-rich blood to the muscles that are doing the work of running. During this effort, stress is increased in all of the cardiopulmonary organs.

The adaptation of muscle cells to a stress level that is applied will result in an increase of strength that is proportional to the stress. Training to run fast for long periods of time involves a systematic increase in the level of stress, as well as allowing muscle cells to adapt during rest. The decline in muscle power as individuals age can be reduced by putting more emphasis on stimulating the central nervous system to cause muscles to learn to react with quick-and-forceful actions, which then can be carried out over a designated period of time.

Neuromuscular characteristics are key components in racing any distance. Quick feet are as important in the 5k as they are in the 100 meters. An endurance runner whose muscles are capable of fast force production, with rapid, well-coordinated, explosive contractions, has a definite edge in racing, given that racing velocity is inversely proportionate to foot-strike time. The less time the foot is in contact with the surface, the faster the race time.

Foot-strike time is a function of how quickly the muscles react to surface impact, how gastrocnemius and anterior tibialis muscles stabilize the ankle controlling dorsiflexion and plantar flexion, and how fast the foot can leave the surface during the stance phase. Quick feet are extremely important in racing, yet are almost totally ignored as a coaching tool. It is important then to create as much neuromuscular power as possible.

The two major aspects of creating neuromuscular power are running skills and functional muscle strengthening. With proper coaching in these areas, an endurance runner can improve their basic performance speed. Basic performance speed is the single most important physiological variable in determining how fast someone can race at any distance. With correct frontside and backside running mechanics, an athlete can position the feet to strike the running surface as far back under the center of mass as possible, causing a quick on and off the surface foot-strike, while keeping a turnover at 97 per minute. Functional strengthening of the muscles that do the work of running will cause them to become more fatigue-resistant and greatly improve speed endurance.

Creating neuromuscular power is equally as important to racing in all endurance events as it is in creating cardiovascular power. Possessing a high VO_2max and lactate threshold running velocity will not produce the complete runner. These physiological attributes must be complemented by complete neuromuscular development, if a runner is going to hold a race pace, cover surges, and be able to answer the finishing kicks of other runners.

Seven-Part Guideline for a Successful Training Season

❑ *Part #1: Running Efficiency/Gold Medal Running Form*

Since running is a neural thing and is controlled by the central nervous system, all runners can adapt their running technique become a more effective competitor. The foot has evolved into a very practical lever, with the frontal part being flexible and elastic. The manner in which the foot strikes the running surface is a key factor in fast and efficient running. During the stride cycle, coaches must teach the runner's knee to be driven forward and the thigh extended to its most forward and upper position.

This action allows the lower leg and foot to be brought back under the runner's center of gravity with a claw-back action. When this sequence happens, it causes a mid-foot touchdown, putting the entire foot in contact with the surface. This ballistic movement creates a great force, without undue stress on the limbs of the lower leg. With a mid-foot landing, the first contact is at a point just in front of the heel bone, slightly to the outside.

As the weight of the runner's body collapses the flexible part of the foot, the weight moves slightly to the inside, causing some degree of pronation. As the weight of the body moves ahead of the fulcrum of the foot, the weight shifts slightly to the outside, resulting in a supination action. When the center of mass moves ahead of the collapsed foot, it snaps back to its original configuration. These actions literally screw the foot into the surface, creating great forward force.

The claw-back action requires great strength in the core and hamstring muscles. This action can only be achieved by teaching the neuromuscular system to perform this act. A mental image of an Olympic champion runner provides a snapshot of how the runner should look. A tall, upright torso, with the arms hanging loosely from the shoulders, and bent approximately at a 90-degree angle, is a must for efficient running. In order to keep the torso in a strong, upright posture throughout the race or vigorous workout, a runner must possess strong core muscles. An endurance athlete's running rhythm, the best combination of stride rate and stride length, determines the speed with which they can run a race in its entirety.

❑ *Part #2: Functional Muscle Strength—Neuromuscular Power*

By doing running-specific strength activities, a runner's maximal running speed can be enhanced through an increase in neuromuscular power. The greater an individual's maximal running velocity, the higher a runner's performance speed at any distance raced. In particular, as a person's maximal running speed increases, their 800, 1500, 3k, 5k, and 10k race performance will improve. Neuromuscular training improves a runner's basic performance speed. Basic performance speed for endurance racing relates to a person's 400-meter speed. In order for an endurance athlete to maintain a fast and efficient running velocity throughout an entire race or workout, the athlete must strengthen the muscles that do the work of running in a running-specific manner.

Traditional weight training falls short of accomplishing this because most weight training is performed in a non-upright position. Functional running strength begins with using a person's own bodyweight as resistance. As the athlete gains strength and improves running velocities, dumbbells and medicine balls can then be used to increase resistance.

❏ *Part #3: Lactate Tolerance—Lactate Shuttle*

When running speeds reach a velocity where lactate levels begin to build up faster in the blood stream than can be shuttled back to energy, the runner has reached a lactate threshold. Lactate is a major muscle fuel. Accordingly, the runner's lactate threshold sets the parameter for continued muscular functioning. If lactate threshold occurs at slower running speeds, the muscles are not prepared for intense running velocities. If, on the other hand, the muscles can work at higher velocities, you have a higher lactate threshold.

❏ *Part #4: $\dot{V}O_2max$*

The physiological variable that is at the center of a runner's improvement in race performance is $\dot{V}O_2max$. $\dot{V}O_2max$ is the minimum velocity at which maximal aerobic capacity is obtained. This important variable reveals both the magnitude of our aerobic capacity and the efficiency with which an individual moves, when running at a high intensity. $\dot{V}O_2max$ is an excellent predictor of a person's ability to race in distances from 800 meters through the marathon.

❏ *Part #5: Speed Endurance*

Runners should try to improve their ability to hold a fast pace for longer periods of time. For example, they could run intervals at an 800- and 1500-meter pace, with controlled rest. They should run these intervals fast enough to quickly flood the bloodstream with lactate, so that the muscles can learn to convert it back to energy (e.g., 50m, 100m, 150m, etc. intervals).

❏ *Part #6: Mind Over Matter*

The brain sets the parameters for pain tolerance. When the muscles reach a point of exertion previously unattained while training, the brain tells them to back off and conserve the expenditure of energy. It is this protective mechanism that must be overcome both by the will of the athlete and through specific training undertaken by the athlete in order to maximize the development of the key physiological factors. The athlete must learn to eliminate negative thoughts and overcome any mental restraints that might exist. Not only can proper workouts help eliminate the psychological barriers that might otherwise arise in competition, it can also extend an athlete's pain barrier even higher.

❏ *Part #7: Race-Specific Preparation*

Regardless of the distance of the race, each distance has specific preparation that must be made if a runner is to achieve optimal race results. The most important factor is to make sure the previous six physiological variables have been properly addressed. If an individual has performed their workouts at both their current race pace, as well as their next-goal pace, they are not ready to improve their performance. A runner's combination of workouts must address all of the aforementioned six physiological variables.

CHAPTER 7 ━━━━━━━━━━━━
Racing

The ability of a human being to race in distances of 800 meters through the marathon is dependent upon several factors, including each individual's genetic ability to maximize speed, running economy, $v\dot{V}O_2max$, $\dot{V}O_2max$, lactate conversion, and mental toughness. In order to maximize $\dot{V}O_2max$ and the conversion of lactate back to energy, the athlete must train the cardiovascular system to produce a strong heart and a capillary circulatory system that can send large amounts of oxygen-rich blood to the muscles that do the work of running, as well as teach the muscular system to recycle lactic acid (lactate).

Speed, running economy, and mental toughness are products of the neuromuscular system and make neural training an essential part of any scheme of training humans to race in endurance events. The key to training to race in endurance events is to teach the human body to run fast for prolonged periods of time. The athlete who can hold the fastest pace over measured distances of 800 meters, 1500 meters, the mile, 3k, 5k, 10k, and marathon will win those races. Accordingly, all training schemes should begin with establishing a base that facilitates the enhancement of speed, running economy, $v\dot{V}O_2max$, $\dot{V}O_2max$, lactate thresholds, and the mental aspects of racing.

From a long-term development perspective, all of these areas of training are most effective when undertaken concurrently with periods of concentrated training effort dedicated to the specificity of the race distances, as compared to a gradual buildup, with a mileage quota. Building a base through a gradual buildup of mileage, and then trying to incorporate greater intensities in the training workloads, will result in fewer capillaries and mitochondria, as well as lower $\dot{V}O_2max$, when compared to running faster velocities from the beginning of the training period.

Instead of building a base, beginning with six to eight weeks of moderate running velocities, the runner will achieve greater capillary development and better waste disposal in that time period by beginning with short segments of multi-tiered intensities that include speed work, 800 meters, 1500 meters, 3k, 5k, and 10k paces. These intensities should be undertaken concurrently with functional muscle strengthening and performing running-skill drills, which will greatly enhance $\dot{V}O_2max$. Learning to run with power and efficiency is a key aspect of improving $\dot{V}O_2max$.

When athletes run races, in general, they do not run at some arbitrary level of intensity. The percentage of $\dot{V}O_2max$ that they can sustain for a specific amount of time is predictable. For example, research has shown that 100 percent $\dot{V}O_2max$ can be sustained for only about 8 to 10 minutes in trained runners. Talented, highly trained runners race 3k at about 98 to 100 percent of $\dot{V}O_2$max; 5km at about 90 to 95 percent of $\dot{V}O_2$max; and a marathon at about 80 to 85 percent of $\dot{V}O_2$max.

An athlete's $\dot{V}O_2$max can be improved with mileage and speed work. The more trained the athletes are, the more important the intensity of training becomes to improve their $\dot{V}O_2$max. $\dot{V}O_2$max has been shown to plateau after three weeks of daily training. In other words, their training stimulus needs to increase about every three weeks to improve their $\dot{V}O_2$max further.

There does not seem to be any further increase in $\dot{V}O_2$max with more than about 70 to 75 miles per week, unless more intense training is added. Research has shown that high-intensity training (95 to 120 percent $\dot{V}O_2$max) is the optimal stimulus for improving $\dot{V}O_2$max. Long intervals (two to five) minutes are the most potent stimulus, because athletes repeatedly reach and sustain their $\dot{V}O_2$max during the work periods. Short intervals of up to one-minute, however, can also improve $\dot{V}O_2$max, as long as they are performed at a high level of intensity and with short, active recovery periods to keep $\dot{V}O_2$max elevated throughout the workout. Regardless of the length of the intervals chosen, athletes should run intervals at the speed at which $\dot{V}O_2$max occurs (referred to as the "velocity at $\dot{V}O_2$max"), which is approximately 3000 meter-race pace.

The following examples illustrate several specific $\dot{V}O_2$max workouts:
- 5 x 1k m at v$\dot{V}O_2$max, with a 1 to 1 work-to-rest ratio
- 6 x 800 meters at v$\dot{V}O_2$max, with a 1 to 1 work-to-rest ratio
- 40 x 200 meters at v$\dot{V}O_2$max, with a 1 to 1 work-to-rest ratio

Although $\dot{V}O_2$max is considered an aerobic variable, the speed at which $\dot{V}O_2$max occurs involves a considerable contribution from oxygen-independent (anaerobic) metabolism, since it occurs at a speed faster than the lactate threshold. The fastest rate of oxygen use occurs when there is also energy being produced without oxygen. Even though it is tempting to run faster when the intervals are shorter, the pace should be the same for all three of the aforementioned workouts, since the goal is the same—to improve $\dot{V}O_2$max. As athletes progress, their workouts should be made more challenging by adding more repetitions or decreasing the recovery period, rather than by running faster. The pace of the workouts should only be increased once the athlete's race times have shown that they are indeed faster.

Among the guidelines that should be used to develop a complete runner are the following:
- Incorporate running skills and functional muscle strengtheners into the warm-up and cool down.
- Learn to run with efficient and powerful foot strikes (i.e., Gold Medal running form).
- Learn to relax while running fast. Run as fast as possible, while staying completely relaxed.

- Use functional strengthening activities to condition the muscles that do the work of running and prepare them to withstand both dynamic and ballistic running. Strengthen the entire body, since upper body and core strength play an important role in efficient running. Functional-strengthening activities help the working muscles to become fatigue-resistant, as well as help prevent injuries. Without sufficient strength and flexibility, injuries are inevitable.
- Use short, fast intervals that not only quickly flood the muscle cells with lactate, they also recruit faster-twitch muscle fibers from the very beginning.
- Use intervals at v$\dot{V}O_2$max, lasting 30 seconds to three to five minutes, with a 1:1 rest.
- Use circuit work that combines intervals at v$\dot{V}O_2$max pace and functional strength activities.
- Use fartlek running, when building volume.
- Use hills and other resistant running to develop more power.

Correct Running Mechanics

Athletes should be aware that correct running mechanics are vital to developing their speed potential. When running, the foot should make first contact on its flexible part, as far back under the center of mass as possible, while traveling in a backward motion. Making the foot strike the ground on the flexible part and as far back under the runner's center of mass creates the most force and helps make running as economical as possible. Always land on the flexible part of the foot, never the heel. Start running with short, easy strides, progressively adding intensity as the muscles warm up. Recruit the abs and do not tense the legs, while running. Let them feel as if they were hanging loosely from pivot points in the hip. Relax the quads. If an athlete feels like the glutes are doing the work, they are running correctly.

Runners should never try to extend their stride with big, lunging gallops. Instead, they should take medium-length, quick strides and focus on keeping the foot strike under the center of mass. They should use a high heel follow-through, cycling the leg around for the next stride, putting the foot in position for a quick and forceful claw-back action. Correct running form features a tall, upright, relaxed torso, held directly over the hips, with the arms hanging loosely from the shoulders.

Fast Running

Maximizing the recovery and touchdown, along with a quick foot strike, are the critical aspects of fast running. The upper-leg speed at touchdown is the most important factor, since it affects both the amount of braking and the amount of ground contact time. Decreasing ground contact time is the means by which runners maximize their stride rate. As such, properly preparing the leg for touchdown is a critical movement.

A runner's frontside mechanics should entail several factors. For example, when the foot pushes off the surface, the lead knee and thigh drive forward and upward. When the knee reaches its most forward position, the lower leg and foot are quickly brought back under the center of mass, making first contact on the flexible part of the foot.

A runner's backside mechanics are also important. For example, as the big toe pushes off the ground, the heel is immediately driven up and under the buttocks. As the drive leg goes forward, the heel steps over the support leg just above the knee, placing it in position for a powerful foot strike. The arms are held at approximately a 90-degree angle, with the muscles of the upper body as relaxed as possible.

The predominate factor in faster running is the ability to generate and transform muscular force to the running surface. Turnover and stride length, along with good frontside and backside running mechanics, produce the force that the foot creates upon contact with a running surface. The greater the force, the greater the body's ability to overcome gravity. Gravity keeps pulling the athlete back to earth and must continually be counteracted as the individual runs. The major component of gravity is mass. All factors considered, the greater the mass equals greater gravitational pull.

A commonly held belief is that the horizontal direction of the stride is where the power is directed. A study published in the *Journal of Biomechanics* in 1987 showed the amount of force used horizontally during constant speed running is as little as one-tenth the amount of force that is applied vertically. This factor is also substantiated in Dr. Ralph Mann's *The Mechanics of Sprinting.*

During constant speed running, disregarding air resistance, propulsion and breaking forces are equal. Accordingly, the amount of force applied to the running surface to propel the body horizontally is offset by the braking force, when the foot contacts the running surface again. The best way to oppose gravity is with proper running mechanics. This factor requires a knee-up, toe-up, and ankles-over-knee running action that brings the foot as far back under the center of mass as possible. The farther back under the center of mass that a runner's foot can strike the running surface, the more power that is created. This scenario is accomplished by correct mechanics and running-specific strengthening exercises for the quads, buttocks, and hamstring muscles. The best way to increase stride length and turnover is by increasing the power of the working muscles, not the other way around.

Speed is the product of dynamic strength and the ability to produce force when the body's limbs are moving at a high velocity. Genetically gifted athletes have the ability to maintain the level of strength to a greater degree as their speed of movement increases. Eccentric-muscle contraction (a type of muscle activation that increases tension on the muscle as it lengthens, e. g., the act of standing from a sitting position) is greatly involved in developing speed. All factors considered, genetically gifted athletes have the ability to produce a greater strength increment as the speed of eccentric movement increases.

Through training, runners must enhance their strength endurance potential. As the length of the race increases, strength endurance becomes a critical factor on the body's ability to handle accumulating waste products. It also becomes a deciding factor in performance.

Correct running mechanics are vital to developing an athlete's speed potential. The development of the skills of running plays a very important role in speed enhancement and the ability to produce power. Running movements, which tend to be learned through early experience with the act of running, are often detrimental to learning to run fast. Speed can be greatly improved through learned actions of the body's levers.

Speed work enhances the physiological aspects of endurance. Recent research indicates that sprint-type training is linked with major benefits for endurance runners. Basic performance speed and LT running velocity are two reliable predictors of endurance racing potential. Sprint work can increase maximal running speed and LT running velocity, as well as enhance $\dot{V}O_2$max and $v\dot{V}O_2$max.

Researchers in England and Australia have discovered that a unique protein, a special muscle-membrane bound, monocarboxylate transporter called MCTl, which captures free lactate molecules and pulls them into the mitochondria of the muscle cell, where lactate can be converted to fuel for exercise. Increased concentrations of MCTl enhance greater fatigue-resistance, as well as LT running velocity. MCTl concentrations are increased through sprint training.

Sprint training not only increases basic speed, but also lifts LT, increases the production of aerobic enzymes and expands the blood flow to muscle cells. All runners can benefit from sprint training. Sprint training should not be confused with speed development. While sprint work is only a small part of speed-enhancement training, it fills a gap in training athletes to compete in endurance races.

Endurance Running Is Three-Dimensional

The shorter the race, the closer the runner comes to maintaining top speed. As the distance of the race increases, the lower the percentage of top speed that can be held in its entirety. The faster a person's basic speed, the greater the potential for racing at any distance. In races of 800 meters and longer, endurance plays a major role. The average velocity that can be maintained at any specific distance is referred to as an individual's speed-endurance index. Running speed can be broken down into the following categories: acceleration 0 to 40 meters—true speed; 40 to 80 meters—average basic performance speed; running at a 300-meter velocity for 400 meters—basic speed-endurance velocity.

One Step at a Time

Running is accomplished by moving forward one step at a time, using a springy action made possible by elastic springs in the feet and legs. Energy is stored during each foot strike and released at toe-off, making the act of running energy efficient. To become an accomplished runner, an individual must move forward with a coordinated combination of stride length and stride frequency of the lower limbs, with balance and stabilization assistance from the upper limbs and core. The neural system is in command of all of the muscular actions that are involved in running. An inability by the neural system to maintain balance limits the capacity for optimum stride length, especially when running at mid-to-maximum running velocities, i.e., $\dot{V}O_2$max running velocities.

Sensor input from the central nervous system will, in effect, regulate stride length and stride frequency. During an endurance race, the body continues to struggle for balance and stability. When the center of mass passes over the support limb, the body must maintain dynamic equilibrium, i.e., a tall erect torso, with the head, shoulders, and hips in a line directly over the collapsed support foot. The perfect model for demonstrating this position is the Ethiopian Olympic gold medalist Haile Gebrselassie.

As an endurance runner becomes more efficient through training, running economy improves. Through running, the body develops its own combination of stride length and frequency in its effort to achieve a desired velocity. Dr. Ralph Mann has demonstrated, through high-speed motion analysis studies, that too much time in the air and too much time on the ground hinder velocity movement. He has also found that reducing foot contact time by as little as a 1/100 of a second produces marked improvement in races of any distance, primarily because reducing foot strike time improves stride rate (turnover).

To a degree, foot-strike time, turnover time, and heel cycle determine race times. A lack of functional running strength to maintain a rhythmical stride length that is compatible with the desired turnover time leads to overstriding and an inefficient use of energy. Training the trunk to achieve balance, correct arm action, and proper foot strike are learned through performing running skill drills and running-specific strength activities. While improving maximal aerobic power is of utmost importance in the development of an athlete's ability to race in endurance events, running alone will not develop maximal neuromuscular power.

American coaches and athletes need to understand that running is first a neural thing and that coaching the neuromuscular system can no longer be ignored. They must come to the understanding that aerobic power and neuromuscular power must be developed concurrently, not separately.

The neural system coordinates muscular contractions. Research indicates that the athlete who wants to run more quickly must teach the nervous system not only to stimulate the muscles that create greater force in a shorter period of time, but also to improve the manner in which the nervous system integrates muscular activity. Muscles that create propulsive force must be stimulated at just the right time, while muscles that might restrict movement must be relaxed at the proper moment. Muscles will not automatically do this and must be coached to respond to the commands of the nervous system.

Running mile after mile at moderate velocities is not neural training. In fact, it is a detriment to fast running, because it does not promote the ability of the nervous system to generate a high level of muscular force. Even more problematic, it retards basic genetic speed. Neural training should feature quick, forceful movements and places a high premium on coordinating muscular activity in the most efficient manner possible. Quick forceful contractions are desirable for endurance runners, if they expect to reach their optimal race performance.

To paraphrase a biblical saying, the body cannot exist on bread alone. All factors considered, there has to be some grape juice flowing through the veins. An individual cannot become a complete runner through running alone. Athletes have to supplement their aerobic power development with dynamic warm-ups and circuit training that promote functional leg strength and quick-foot strikes. If coaches would allot 30 percent of practice time to developing the neuromuscular aspects of running, they would be totally amazed at the improvement in race performance in their athletes that would occur. Such a schedule would still allow 70 percent of workout time to the development of aerobic power. The underlying message that should be emphasized in this regard is straightforward:

> *We need to stop thinking about a mileage quota and let the number of miles run per week be a result of carefully planned workouts that are dedicated to developing the complete runner.*

Coaches at all competitive levels continue to persist on developing an aerobic base through a build-up of mileage before adding elements that form a foundation for any of the other physiological variables of endurance training. The overriding problem with this way of thinking is that by the time an aerobic base is accomplished, it is too late in the season to efficiently establish a foundation for speed, fatigue-resistant muscle strengthening, and other variables of training.

The other issue with the theory of addressing an athlete's aerobic base before any other variable is that while running the mega miles at moderate velocity, the athletes, left to their own means, almost without exception will develop a slow foot strike that promotes overstriding. This situation leads to a heel-first touchdown and a braking action with every step. During the aerobic base period, neuromuscular patterns that are detrimental to speed development are firmly established in the central nervous system. All factors considered, these patterns cannot be changed to a significant degree during the period of speed training.

Coaches who are successful at the regional, state, and national level often argue that aerobic base first and a mileage quota works for them, so why change? They fail to consider the fact that since everyone else is using the same training scheme, any success they achieve is because of their ability to accumulate greater numbers of athletes and motivate them to work harder than the athletes on other teams/squads.

In essence, it is typically the coach's personality and ability to recruit athletes to the program and then motivate them to work hard that makes for a successful program. Coaches who can attract large numbers of athletes to the program are highly successful, because the more bodies that are training the better the percentage for finding athletes who are genetically gifted enough to perform well. It is doubtful that any coach at the youth, high school, or collegiate level has the development of an Olympic caliber athlete as their major coaching goal. It is through these ranks, however, that such athletes emerge.

Unfortunately, when American elite endurance runners compete against the elite athletes of other nations, they often find themselves woefully unprepared to answer the surges that occur during a race and the finishing kicks that transpire at the end. Arguably, the main reason that the elite runners of America cannot match the speed of other international athletes is that no one ever taught them how to run fast. American coaches at all levels are so consumed with developing cardio power that they virtually ignore the importance of neuromuscular power. As a result, they do not accord the development of a base for speed its proper priority for racing in endurance events.

Coaches are very traditional; they coach the way that they were coached or trained. Mostly, to their peril, they tend to ignore the published scientific research that is available that shows the importance of speed development, fatigue-resistant functional muscle strength, and the fundamentals of running technique. As a result, the counterproductive cycle of overlooking the need to train the body's neural system continues.

CHAPTER 8
The Role of Speed in Endurance Running

The fact that speed, or the lack thereof, is the greatest single physiological variable that determines a runner's ability to race fast has been documented by scientific research. Dr. Ralph Mann has shown through high tech film analysis that most American endurance runners exhibit too much backside action in their running mechanics and not enough frontside action, when compared to the best world-class runners. Frontside mechanics are the actions that take place after toe-off, while backside mechanics occur after touchdown to the point where the free ankle crosses the support leg.

Too much action behind the center of mass makes it virtually impossible to create maximum power with each foot strike, because the foot cannot be in position to strike the surface far enough back under the center of mass. This situation results in a heel-first foot strike and more braking action with each step. The typical high school endurance athlete runs with 20 percent frontside and 80 percent backside mechanics. In comparison, college-level runners are generally at 30 and 70 percent, while elite runners use 40 percent front side and 60 percent backside action.

Too much backside mechanics is a learned neuromuscular response to high mileage running, with little regard to foot strike and turnover rate. Every step taken when running helps to ingrain a pattern of stride rate and the amount of time that the foot stays on the running surface.

A turnover of 97 per minute, 1.64 per second, is ideal for developing running economy, as well as the ultimate power production for endurance runners. The key to developing an efficient and powerful stride is to engage in drills that teach the working muscles to bring the foot back as far under the center of mass as possible with each step. Stride length has little to do with the height of the runner or the length of the leg. Rather, it has a great deal to do with the velocity with which the runner is moving. By running with a turnover of 97 per minute, an athlete can hold race pace at any distance from 800 meters and would be greater than in longer races, because the center of mass is moving forward at a greater rate.

To answer surges during a race, the runner needs to pick up the turnover to 100 to 104 per minute for the duration of the surge. Surges seldom last more than 20 seconds and require little additional expenditure of aerobic energy. A finishing kick, however, can last from 30 to 60 seconds, requiring competitors to increase their turnover to 104 to 108 per minute. Kicking by increasing the stride length only and keeping the same turnover rate consumes more energy and often results in failure.

The traditional formula for running speed is speed = stride length x stride rate. Runners with a faster turnover (stride, rate, time) will run faster than when they took steps less frequently. For example, a turnover of 97 per minute compared to 90 per minute. A runner who can increase a stride length, a distance factor, while keeping the same turnover, can also increase running speed. Runners who can do both of the aforementioned, will definitely increase their speed. These three components of faster running are actually "effect."

A predominate factor in faster running is the ability to generate and transmit muscular force to the running surface. Turnover and stride length, along with good frontside and backside running mechanics, produce the force that the foot creates upon contact with a running surface. The greater the force, the greater the body's ability to overcome gravity. Gravity keeps pulling the athlete back to earth and must continually be counteracted as the individual runs. The major component of gravity is mass, and the greater the mass, the greater the gravitational pull.

A commonly held belief is that the horizontal direction of the stride is where the power is directed. When the foot that is applying the force can be brought backward faster than the center of mass is moving forward, the runner's speed will increase. The rate at which the power foot is being brought backward determines the individual's running velocity. When the foot strike can no longer maintain a rate that is equal to the forward movement of the body, the runner will begin to slow.

Speed work contributes two key adaptations: one is a reduced rate at which glycogen is burned, and the other is a reduction of the buildup of lactate during strenuous effort. Studies show that a decrease in the rate at which glycogen is burned during running promotes stamina, because more glycogen fuel remains in the tank to be utilized after any specific duration of effort. In turn, a diminished buildup of lactate can indicate that lactate is being used efficiently for energy. It is being broken down, instead of accumulating in the muscles.

Increasing the functional strength of the working muscles not only makes them stronger, but also makes them more resistant to fatigue. Activities for functional leg muscle strength can be incorporated into the warm-up and cool-down phase of a training session. Among the functional strengthening activities that an athlete can perform are: leg swings, feet-up, step-ups and squats, vertical hops, walking squats, bounding, spring running, power running, one-leg quick hops and long hops, and double-leg and single-leg hurdle hops.

Endurance development begins with any activity that causes the heart to accelerate its beating rhythm. For runners, this objective is achieved mainly through running workouts. The more intense the workout, the greater its effect on the aerobic development.

Speed development involves adhering to proper running mechanics, which decreases the amount of energy and strength needed to run at a specific velocity and makes a race performance more effective by delaying the onset of fatigue. Training provides the means by which athletes develop their endowed potential. Running mechanics is one of the critical areas to be improved through training.

Strength endurance is a factor because the muscles tend to tire in the final stages of a race or workout. To avoid slowing when the foot makes contact with the running surface, the foot must be moving downwards as fast as possible at the contact point. If a runner cannot produce a backward-foot speed equal to the forward-body velocity, the foot will receive a negative push or braking action. More than any other factors, the strength of the hamstring and gluteus muscles dictate the degree of success in racing.

Quality

Enhancing neuromuscular strength and cardiovascular strength concurrently is essential to being able to do the highest percentage quality work. The stronger the muscles that do the work of running, the stronger the heart. The stronger the heart, the stronger the working muscles. Running skills and running-specific strength exercises can readily be incorporated into the warm-up and cool-down phases of a practice. An example of a running workout that can elicit considerable aerobic and anaerobic benefits is to run as far as possible, while staying completely relaxed for 60 seconds, alternating with three minutes of relatively easy running performed to complete exhaustion. Running at a 10k goal-pace will greatly enhance LTRV.

Improving Basic Speed

The process of improving an individual's level of basic speed begins with programming the athlete's neuromuscular system to produce dynamic and explosive foot strikes and turnover. This development can be accomplished with the use of a speed-agility ladder and acceleration ladders, along with performing other quick-foot drills.

A speed-agility ladder, which is set with 14" spacing, lays flat on the surface. The training begins with the athlete walking through the ladder, exhibiting a tall, relaxed posture, while using short quick arm action. The 14" spacing causes the foot to land under the center of mass.

Initially, the foot makes contact on its flexible part. When the entire foot is on the surface of the ground, the athlete lifts the heel and then pushes off with the toes, causing a rolling action. When the toes leave the surface, the athlete steps one ankle over the other and quickly places the other foot in position. The athlete should begin the activity with an easy tempo and then repeat with medium effort, and, finally, walk as quickly as possible while maintaining good posture.

When exiting the ladder, the athlete should return, walking backward, pushing off with the toes. The next phase is to complete this action while running. The objective is to teach the neuromuscular system to produce a quick on-and-off-the-surface foot action.

Another drill is to step one foot quickly into each space, followed by the other foot, and then step forward and out. The athlete should advance through the ladder with this two-in, two-out, quick-foot action. The individual should complete two lengths facing forward, two moving left, and two moving right. The next progression is to run with quick-foot action, using three-foot spacing, e.g., hash marks.

Then, the athlete should advance to the acceleration ladder. Flat sticks or lines drawn in the dirt with proper spacing can also be used in the activity. Running the patterns previously detailed for the acceleration ladder will help the athlete develop gold medal running form. During the first 30 meters of activity, the individual should concentrate on quick-foot acceleration. On the next 30 meters, the focus should be on the knee-up, toe-up running positions, and during the final 30 meters, on an ankle-over-knee and high-heel follow-through.

As previously noted, speed must be taught, beginning with the very first practice of the season. While anyone can improve their basic speed, it takes hours and hours of diligent practice, using drills and functional-muscle strengthening activities. Running fast intervals will improve an individual's race times by improving their ability to hold a pace that is closer to a specific percentage of their basic speed for a longer period of time. In other words, for example, with proper training, a person can eventually run a 10k at their present 5k race pace.

Improving pure speed can only come from conditioning the neuromuscular system to produce faster contractions that lend to more dynamic and forceful foot strikes. The neuromuscular system is like a computer. An individual puts in certain data, and it will spit out an answer.

Coaches should begin their speed orientation by teaching their athletes to learn how to run with gold medal form. To the degree possible, an effort must be made to emulate the running action of gold medal winners at the World and Olympic Games. As such, runners should be required to maintain a tall upright posture, with their head and shoulders directly above their hips. Furthermore, they should exhibit quick, but relaxed, arm action and a medium length stride, with a fast turnover and quick foot strike.

Their frontside mechanics should entail a knee-up, toe-up that allows for a quick downward drive of the foot. The foot should strike the surface as far back under the center of mass as possible, causing a mid-foot touchdown. When the foot pushes off the running surface, the heel should be quickly driven directly upward and then under the buttocks, forming a short lever, with the foot crossing the support leg slightly above the knee. This action prepares the foot to be in position for another quick and forceful foot strike.

The muscles that cause this action are the quads, hamstrings, buttocks, and core. Through running-specific strengthening activities, these muscles can be made both strong and fatigue-resistant, a result that will not only allow the runner to hold a fast race pace, but also be able to answer surges and respond to the finishing speed of other athletes. Learning to run with power and efficiency begins with a tall, relaxed posture that places the head and shoulders directly over the hips. The ability to manufacture a relaxed upper body, with short, quick-arm action, is essential for fast-relaxed running.

Arm Drills

❑ *Drill #1*

Assume a running posture with the arms hanging loosely from the shoulders Swing the fully extended arms back and forth with no help from the shoulders muscles. Drive the arms in a full range of motion, while allowing them to break slightly at the top and lengthen slightly at the bottom. Increase the tempo of the arm swing, while staying completely relaxed. Accelerate the arm action until they begin to tighten then stop and start over. Repeat six times.

❑ *Drill #2*

Stand tall, with a relaxed torso, allowing the arms to hang freely from the shoulders. Close the hands loosely, with the thumb nails pointing upward. Bend the arms and bring the hands to the top of the hips, with the elbows forward, stopping the hands at mid-line of the chest, then drive the elbows backward stopping the hands at the top of the hips. Accelerate this action for 10 seconds, six times. Practice this drill in front of a mirror, making sure the facial muscles stay relaxed.

❑ *Drill #3*

Begin running lightly in place landing on the flexible part of the fact with quick, relaxed arms movement. Gradually increase the running tempo, while bringing the foot higher and higher up under the center of mass. Continue increasing the tempo until the runner can no longer stay relaxed.

❑ *Drill #4*

Progression of running: Assume a running posture. Begin the arm action, while marking time with the feet. Continue this action, while inching forward by lifting the heel and pushing off with the toes. Begin running with quick-foot action, while stepping one ankle over the other. Continue running action, while stepping the ankle over the opposite mid-shin (calf). Continue running, advancing to the ankle over the knee. Walk for 10 seconds and then repeat for 10 minutes. Running action is an underneath movement, not a forward movement.

❑ *Drill #5*

This drill involves using the speed agility ladder. Walk through the ladder with a quickstep action by lifting the heel and stepping one ankle over the other. Complete the ladder six times, while trying to walk faster each time. Maintain quick arm action and relaxed upper body.

Sprint Training

Sprint training improves the buffering capacity and upgrades s runner's performance during exertions that rely primarily on aerobic metabolism. Research suggests that reasonable amounts of high intensity might be optional during the base-building phase. Even beginners can do small amounts of sprint work. Beginning with moderate running velocities and then gradually increasing the intensity throughout the training season does not prepare the muscles to race at high intensities.

Sprint training enhances the buffering capacity of muscles, which produces an affect that usually promotes better tolerance to high-intensity running, as well as, subsequently, greater endurance at intense paces. The physiological and psychological variables that a training scheme should develop concurringly, in order of development, include the following: speed, maximal running speed, resistance to fatigue, running economy, lactate threshold speed, $\dot{V}O_2$max v$\dot{V}O_2$max, running-specific strength, and training the brain.

❑ *Enhancing the Physiological Aspects of Endurance With Speed Work*

Recent research indicates that sprint-type training is linked with major benefits for endurance runners. For example, basic performance speed and LT running velocity have been found to be two of the most reliable predictors of endurance-racing potential. Furthermore, sprint work can increase maximal running speed and LT running velocity, as well as enhancing $\dot{V}O_2$max and v$\dot{V}O_2$max.

As noted previously, researchers in England and Australia have discovered that a unique protein, a special muscle-membrane bound, monocarboxylate transporter called MCTI. MCTI captures free lactate molecules and pulls them into the mitochondria of the muscle cell, where lactate can be converted to fuel for exercise. Increased concentrations of MTCI enhance greater fatigue-resistance and LT-running velocity. MTCI concentrations are increased through sprint training. Sprint training not only enhances basic speed, it also lifts LT, as well as increases the production of aerobic enzymes and expands the blood flow to muscle cells. All runners can benefit from sprint training. Sprint training should not be confused with speed development. Sprint work is only a small part of speed-enhancement training. In fact, it fills a significant gap in training athletes to compete in endurance races.

The subjects in the aforementioned study were seven male adults, with a background in endurance training. The study involved completing 17 workouts, each of which consisted of four sets of nearly maximal (e.g., 90 to 100 percent effort) sprints, 40 to 100 meters in length. The total number of sprints increased from 14 the first week to 30 the sixth week, with the length of reps increased from 40 to 80 meters, then to 100 meters during the sixth week. The rest/work ratio began at 1:3 and was gradually reduced to 1:1, with recovery between sets kept at four minutes throughout the 42-day period. Sprint sessions were conducted three times per week. A 10-yard build-up to the start line allowed the runners to run fast-relaxed for the test distance.

The first workout session entailed the following:

Set #1: 4 x 40 meters

Set #2: 4 x 50 meters

Set #3: 4 x 60 meters

Set #4: 2 x 80 meters

The final sprint workout (session 18) encompassed the following:

Set #1: 8 x 100 meters

Set #2: 6 x 100 meters

Set #3: 8 x 80 meters

Set #4: 6 x 80 meters

The fitness level of the athletes was determined by a run-to-exhaustion test at 110 percent $\dot{V}O_2max$ velocity at the beginning of the study then again after the 18th workout. At the end of the six weeks of sprint training, the seven athletes improved their running velocity at $\dot{V}O_2max$ ($v\dot{V}O_2max$) by 11 percent.

❑ *Sprint Training With an Acceleration Ladder*

An acceleration ladder can also be used to improve speed and running technique. The first 30 meters is designed to teach foot strike and turnover, while gradually extending stride length. Flat sticks can be employed for the first eight steps with the following settings:

ENGLISH	1'6"	2'	2'6"	3'	3'6"	4'	4'3"*	4'6"*
		3'6"	6'	9'	12'6"	16'6"	20'9"	25'6"
METRIC	.46	.62	.77	.92	1.07	1.27	1.30	1.38
		1.08	1.85	2.77	3.84	5.1	6.4	7.79

*Note: Use 3" risers to complete 30 meters.

ENGLISH	4'9"	5'	5'	5'	5'	5'	5'	5'
	5'	5'	5'	5'	5'	5'	30'3"	33'3"
	40'3"	45'3"	50'3"	55'3"	60'3"	65'3"	70'3"	75'3"
	80'3"	85'3"	90'3"	95'3"				
METRIC	1.46	1.54	1.54	1.54	1.54	1.54	1.54	1.54
	9.25	11.19	12.73	14.27	15.8	17.35	18.9	20.43
	21.967	23.5	25.5	26.6	28.3	29.7		

*Note: The spacing for the next 15 meters, which emphasize knee drive, with dorsiflexion of the ankles and a forceful foot stri.ke, remains at 5' or 1.54m with 5" risers.

ENGLISH	100'3"	105'3"	110'3"	115'3"	120'3"	125'3"	130'3"	135'3"	140'3"	145'3"
METRIC	30.84	32.38	33.9	35.46	37	38.5	40	41.6	43.15	44.7

The height of the risers should be increased to 7" for the next 15 meters. Runners should maintain their knee drive and dorsiflexion, while cycling the heel through directly under the butt and continuing with a forceful foot strike. Should an athlete's speed improve, the stride length should be increased in 3" increments up to a stride six-feet in length. A stride longer than that would be highly unlikely.

ENGLISH	150'3"	155'6"	160'9"	167'	173'	179'	185'	191'	197'
METRIC	46.2	47.84	49.46	51	53.23	55	56.9	58.76	60.6

Athletes who master the 60-meter ladders can extend their run up to 90 to 100 meters, while maintaining turnover and foot speed from muscle memory. No ladders are employed for these additional meters. Consistent use of the ladders will produce a turnover of 98 per minute, which is consistent with economical running, with proper racing and stride patterns.

Racing and Stride Length

When the gun goes off, the first step should be a short quick one. The runner should then aggressively speed up until the proposed pace for the race is reached. Endurance runners step up their running velocity by increasing both stride length and stride rate, until they reach a velocity of about 57 seconds per 400 meters (7m per second). Above 7m per second, stride rate is entirely responsible for increasing velocity. At a speed of 4m per second (1:40 per 400 meters), the stride length will be about 1.6m, with a stride rate of 2.5 per second. Picking up the tempo to 5m per second (80 per 400), the stride rate will increase to about 2.9 steps per second with a stride length of approximately 1.73m.

Speeding up to 6m per second involves an increase in both stride rate and stride length (stride rate = 3.15; stride length = 1.9m). When a runner's velocity reaches 7m per second, the stride length begins to level off, while the stride rate continues to pick up. At 7m per second, the stride length is about 2.lm, with the stride rate 3.3 per second.

At velocities of 8m per second, the stride length holds at about 2m, while further gains in speed are accomplished through increasing stride rate. At this speed, the stride rate moves up to 3.8 steps per minute (1.9 T.O.) per second or 114 per minute. Picking up the turnover requires decreasing ground-contact time. Ground-contact time, while a running velocity of 9m per second, requires a ground contact time of only 1/100 millisecond. At high speeds, the upper limits in stride length are reached before the lower limit on foot contact time is attained.

Power production is an essential element in decreasing foot contact time. Learned frontside mechanics, as well as learned backside mechanics that places the foot as far back under the center of mass as possible on contact, are the key to a faster foot strike.

Speed Development

Proper running mechanics decreases the amount of energy and strength needed to run at a specific velocity and makes a performance more effective by delaying the onset of fatigue. Training provides the means by which to develop an individual's level of genetic potential strength. Frontside and backside mechanics are additional critical areas that can be improved through training. Strength endurance is a factor, because the muscles tend to tire in the final stages of a race or workout.

The two major characteristics of a proficient coach are knowing how to teach and what to teach. To avoid slowing when the foot makes contact with the running surface, the foot must be moving downward as fast as possible at the contact point. If a runner cannot produce a downward foot speed equal to the forward-body velocity, the foot will receive a negative push or braking action. More than any other factors, this action is affected by the strength of the hamstring and gluteal muscles.

❑ *Force Production*

As discussed in Chapter 6, the ability to generate forward movement is integral to running fast. As noted previously, this factor is essentially a by-product of the amount of vertical force that can be applied. As such, the two most important phases of fast running are touchdown speed and ankle crossover speed.

❑ *Basic Speed*

As detailed in Chapter 6, no factor is more important in an individual's ability to race at any distance than that person's level of basic speed. As noted, a number of options exist for improving basic speed, including developing a greater stride rate and increasing stride length. In that regard, both elements can be enhanced by improving running mechanics (refer to Figure 8-2) and performing functional strength exercises.

While the aforementioned information can be considered very interesting, it does not explain how to train the muscles to improve a person's speed. As noted previously, everything that happens during muscular action is controlled by the central nervous system and that running is carried out by complete neuromuscular actions. Furthermore, when the muscles are stimulated to engage in a specific action, a specific reaction occurs. When humans run, the foot is the body part that hits the surface with each step.

The foot is the lever that applies the culminating force from the stretch power that is stored in the feet, as well as from the muscles and tendons of the buttocks and upper and lower leg. Research conducted by Dr. Ralph Mann, America's foremost expert on sprinting mechanics, details the essence of fast running. According to Dr. Mann, distance runners need to learn to run fast in order to excel in endurance races. In fact, coaches and athletes can take some of Dr. Mann's principles of sprinting and apply them to their training scheme.

Of the various entire specific performance variables, upper-leg rotational speed is the most critical in the production of speed performance. Faster runners maximize their leg recovery and touchdown speed. Figure 8-1 illustrates a tall upright posture, with the foot lever releasing the stored spring energy. Figure 8-2 shows that during an immediate knee-drive action, the foot literally screws itself into the running surface, providing torque and an explosive release of stored stretch power. This action can be taught by walking and then running in a speed ladder, with 14" spacing. Learned frontside mechanics, as well as learned backside mechanics that places the foot as far back under the center of mass as possible on contact, are the key to a faster foot strike.

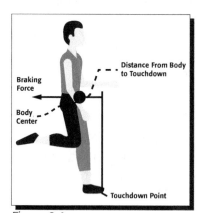

Figure 8-1

Figure 8-2

Energy for Running

The body's primary energy source is adenosine triphosphate, ATP, which comes from the food that we eat. The body's ability to create energy for up to about two minutes is accomplished through a process known as anaerobic glycoses. This process does not depend on oxygen breathed in from the air. This factor being true, a runner can go out-fast for about 90 seconds, without delving into the aerobic pathway of creating energy. At about two minutes, however, it becomes necessary to take in oxygen through breathing to produce energy. At that point, runners settle into their projected race pace. With about 300 to 400 meters to go in the race, a runner can pick up the velocity of the run and forego the aerobic pathway of creating energy and finish with energy from the anaerobic glycolic pathway.

CHAPTER 9

A Training Program for Endurance Running, Based on Skill, Speed, and Strength

When the starting gun goes off, the runner should make their first step a short, quick one. Then, they should aggressively speed up until the proposed pace for the race is reached. As noted previously, endurance runners step up their running velocity by increasing both stride length and stride rate until they reach a velocity of about 57 seconds per 400 meters or seven meters per second. A stride rate above seven meters per second is entirely responsible for improving velocity.

At a speed of four meters per second or 1:40 per 400, the stride length will be about 1.6 meters and the stride rate 2.5 steps per second. Picking up the tempo to five meters per second or 80 seconds per 400, the stride rate will increase to about 2.9 steps per second, with the stride length about 1.73 meters. Speeding up to six meters per second involves an increase of both stride rate and stride length, where the stride rate is 3.15 steps per second and the stride length is 1.9 meters.

When a runner's velocity reaches seven meters per second, the stride length begins to level off, while the stride rate continues to pick up. At seven meters per second, the stride length is about 2.1 meters and the stride rate is 3.3 steps per second. At a velocity of eight meters per second, the stride length stays around 2.1 meters, while further gains in speed are accomplished through increasing the stride rate. At this speed, the stride rate moves up to 3.8 steps per minute or 1.9 turnovers per second or 114 strides per minute.

Improving turnover requires decreasing ground-contact time. Ground-contact time, with a running velocity of nine meters per second, can only be improved by 1/100 millisecond. At fast running speeds, the upper limits in stride length are reached before the lower limit on foot contact time is attained.

Power production is an essential factor in decreasing foot-contact time. Adhering to proper frontside mechanics, as well as to correct backside mechanics that places the foot as far back under the center of mass as possible on contact, is the key to a faster foot strike.

First-time endurance runners and those individuals who are embarking on a new season of training will be limited in their overall work, more by the quick buildup of lactate than by the lack of oxygen consumption. There will be oxygen available for glycolysis, but the lactate shuttle process will not be able to keep up with the conversion of that lactate as quickly as it is produced. This factor puts lactate tolerance near the top of the priorities to determine the sequence of workouts.

While running, no matter what velocity, individuals should always be conscious of their running form. In other words, they need to concentrate on posture and relaxing their arms and shoulders. When on an endurance run, they should not be satisfied with just staying on their projected running pace. As such, they should think about their posture, turnover, relaxation and foot strike. Periodically, they should also check their turnover for a period of 10 seconds. Their goal should be to try for 18 turnovers in 10 seconds.

Gold medal running form includes skill drills that promote a tall, upright posture, with the trunk and head held directly over the hips, the shoulders and arms relaxed, a quick turnover, and a foot strike with a medium-stride length. Short runs of 100 to 150 meters at a fast-relaxed effort are not only great for developing gold medal running form, they will also buildup lactate acid quicker than it can be cycled back to energy.

An individual can enhance their ability to recycle lactate by running short, fast intervals, while at the same time working on their gold medal running form and relaxed running. In this instance, they should begin by running graduated 100 meters, with segments that gradually buildup the intensity of the run. Utilizing 20-meter segments, they should run progressively faster so that they gradually recruit more muscle motor units and bring into play additional Type II fast-twitch fibers. They should ease into the first 20 meters, and then increase their effort to 50 percent for the second 20 meters, 60 percent for the third 20 meters, 70 percent for the fourth 20 meters and finish at 90 percent effort for the last one.

They should perform this workout approximately 10 minutes of actual running time, doing a 100-meter progression run every minute. While undertaking this workout, the lactate will gradually increase, which will stimulate the conversion-to-energy process. During these repeat 100s, the runner should remember to also focus on their posture, relaxation, foot-strike, and turnover.

Since muscles do all of the work of running, it would be advantageous for runners to make their musculature as strong as possible, while adding very little bulk. Running is accomplished mostly through eccentric muscular contraction. Eccentric muscle contraction entails a situation in which a muscle is exerting a force, while attempting to shorten, and yet ends up elongated by other forces acting on it.

Eccentric muscular action, such as running downhill, strains muscles. On the other hand, there is also something about eccentric muscular training that ultimately provides a considerable amount of protection for muscles and tendons. Eccentric muscle contractions recruit more fast-twitch fibers than do concentric contractions, because fast-twitch fibers shorten more quickly than slow-twitch fibers. As a result, an upswing in the stiffness of muscle cells occurs, which allows them to store and utilize impact energy more effectively.

Exercises, such as plyometric exercises cause increases in muscle stiffness. When stiffness increases, the energy cost of running actually decreases. Research indicates that uneconomical runners possess a more compliant running style during ground contact, compared with energy-efficient runners. The key muscles and tendons of running, e.g., the Achilles tendon, calf muscle, patellar, quadriceps, glutei, and hamstrings, are all stretched considerably with each foot strike. If these muscles and tendons are lacking in appropriate stiffness, the leg collapses too much on impact. If the tissues are stiffened up, however, the leg is better able to produce optimal amounts of reactive force. Functional activities to strengthen the muscles, tendons, and ligaments that do the work of running are necessary to create more power and prevent injuries.

All movements in sports are controlled by the central nervous system. Any movement begins in the brain. The brain sends signals to activate the muscle fibers involved in the movement to be performed. The central nervous system controls the intensity and duration of contraction and relaxation of muscle fibers. Competing in endurance racing requires fast and efficient running movements. In many instances, the muscles that perform the work of running are not strong enough to absorb the impact of gravity that occurs with each contact with a running surface. The major issue in this regard is that the muscles are not strengthened concurrently with an increase in intensity and volume of work of training.

Functional muscle strengthening involves activities that mimic the act of running, using an individual's own body weight as the resistance. Examples of such activities are bench step-ups, bench half squats, vertical hops on one leg, and power running. This type of strengthening helps the muscles to create greater power and become more fatigue-resistant. As the body becomes stronger, medicine balls and dumbbells can be used to increase the level of resistance.

The actual act of running is the most overlooked and unappreciated of all factors that allow individuals to race in endurance events. The human foot and its attachments that place it into position to provide power for running are the very essence of running. The foot is an amazing lever that has evolved into the power source for all running. The contour of the foot and its structure of bones, tendons, and ligaments give it a spring-like element that compresses and recoils.

The feet, ankles, bones, and muscles of the lower leg not only absorb the stress of each footfall, but also provide the power for each stride cycle. This duel responsibility demands that these appendages be strong and resilient. Typically, little or no time in a training scheme is allotted to strengthening and conditioning these areas. Most athletes and coaches think that by beginning a season with slow-to-moderate running velocities, they will gradually strengthen the muscles that do the work of running to the degree that they will be adequate to handle the stress when some faster velocities are added. This belief could not be further from the truth, as the incidents of injuries increase dramatically when speed is added to workouts.

Since running is accomplished mostly through eccentric muscular action, these activities should emulate eccentric actions. The major muscles and tendons that provide the strength for absorbing the shock of each footfall are the tibia posterior tendons, anterior tibias tendon, calf muscle, Achilles tendon, and the muscles and tendons in the feet. All of these muscles and tendons stretch, when the center of gravity is directly over the foot on touchdown, thereby creating stretch energy. At toe-off, all of these muscles and tendons spring back to their original position, releasing this stored energy, propelling the body forward.

Injuries to muscles, tendons, and bones from the knee to the toes are the most prevalent and are caused by putting more stress in these areas than the strength of the support muscles can bear. Most injuries in the upper leg and buttocks can also be traced to a weakness in the structure of the lower appendages. In order to prevent or quickly recover from injuries from the hip down to the foot, athletes simply need to systematically increase the level of stress applied on and the subsequent adaption of the muscles involved. Not only will strengthening these muscles and tendons greatly reduce the chance of injury, it will also provide more power with each foot strike. The bottom line is that when muscles are strengthened in a running-specific manner, the risk of injury is minimal, fatigue-resistance is at a high level, and the foundation of speed improvement is made possible.

Speed improvement should be a major goal of any training scheme. Coaches should start their training efforts by teaching everyone how to run using correct running mechanics. This factor should be initiated during the warm-up period and carried on throughout an entire workout. This emphasis is referred to as gold medal running form because the athlete is trying to produce a running form that emulates the World Champions.

The training should be initiated at the beginning of the season with short-rep segments and should work towards a gradual increase of the distance run of each rep. Drills should be performed that enhance the development of speed from the very first day of training and should be continued on a daily basis. Mileage volume should be built up through fartlek-type workouts. Because running slow-to-moderate mileage develops a slow turnover and foot strike, which impedes racing ability, it needs to be avoided.

Furthermore, circuit training should be employed from the beginning of the training season and continued throughout the season. This approach develops overall body strength and enhances the body's ability to convert lactate back to energy. An example of circuit training, in this instance, would be to run four repeat circuits of 400 meters at a 3k-goal pace, alternated with five neuromuscular strengthening activities (discussed in a later chapter). This example illustrates a continuous, nonstop workout, with the intervals run at $v\ddot{V}O_2$max-running velocity.

A Training Program for Endurance Running Based on Skill Speed and Strength

All of the scientific research points to the fact that the periodization of training to race distances of 800 meters-10k should be based on the development of skill, speed, and strength. Speed and strength are far better indicators of a person's potential to race in these events than are endurance factors, such as, $\dot{V}O_2max$. Workouts, emphasizing skill, speed, and strength should address the following:

- Learn how to run with power and efficiency.
- Learn how to run fast-relaxed.
- Learn how to hold the fastest pace possible for as long as possible.
- Learn how to hold a specific race pace for as close to race distance as possible.
- Develop strong fatigue resistant muscles through running specific muscle strengthening.

When all of the aforementioned aspects are addressed, speed, speed endurance, $v\dot{V}O_2max$, $\dot{V}O_2max$, and LTRV will be concurrently developed to the maximum.

Foundation of Training

Forming a foundation for running and racing with running skills, functional leg strength and speed development provides the athlete with the opportunity to run efficiently for relatively long periods of time. Specific competition speeds need to be completed at the lowest fraction of maximal energy cost (i.e., maximum aerobic capacity). As an individual runs, the easier an effort feels, the more room they have to improve their competitive velocity. For example, if a six-minute per mile running velocity is 99 percent of $\dot{V}O_2max$, there is little possibility for that individual to create more energy aerobically. On the other hand, if a person can run a six-minute pace at only 92 percent of their maximum oxygen uptake, they have more potential to improve their racing velocity.

A person's ability to consume oxygen through physical exertion is represented by the symbol $\dot{V}O_2max$. The more oxygen that a person can breathe in and send to the muscles throughout the blood stream, the greater the measure of $\dot{V}O_2max$. Even though $\dot{V}O_2max$ sets the parameters for aerobic power, it is not the best indicator of a person's potential to perform in endurance races. For example, two athletes with the same $\dot{V}O_2max$ rating will probably perform quite differently in an endurance race. The one with better running economy or basic speed will win the race.

The running velocity at which maximal aerobic velocity is attained, however, is a great predictor of racing potential. This running velocity, which is represented by the symbol $v\dot{V}O_2max$, reveals both the magnitude of a person's aerobic capabilities for running and also the efficiency with which the athlete moves when running at very high speeds.

When an individual runs, no aerobic energy can be created, until some anaerobic energy is produced. When muscles break down food to A.T.P. through the process of glycoses, lactic acid (lactate) is a by-product of the burning of oxygen.

The running velocity at which lactate levels begin to pile up in an athlete's blood stream faster than it can be converted back to energy is referred to as their lactate threshold. The improvement of LT running velocity is absolutely essential to running fast for long periods of time. Lactate conversion provides a great muscle fuel. Furthermore, LTRV is the barometer of muscle functions during exercise. If lactate floods the muscles at moderate running speed that individual's muscles are not adequately prepared for high quality efforts. If lactate does not pool in the blood stream until high speeds are reached, the athlete's muscles are doing an excellent job of using lactate as fuel.

When a person's cardio and neural systems are exposed to specific running velocities, both systems will adapt to race at those specific paces. The more that a person trains at a specific velocity, the more efficient they will become at that velocity. Training at multitier velocities will help an athlete become a more complete runner and ensure a high level of fitness. As such, a training scheme must allow for the development of all physiological variables concurrently, as opposed to allotting a specific time period for each one.

It is important for coaches to understand how to teach the body to shuttle lactate back into the muscles for transformation back to energy. The conversion of lactic acid to lactate begins with a chemical process called glucoses. Glucoses is a series of 10 different chemical reactions which break down glucose, a simple six-carbon sugar into a factor called pyruvic acid. The glycolytic conversion of glucose to pyruvic acid quickly provides energy that the muscles need for exercise. For the endurance athlete the most important aspect of glucoses is what happens after the glycolytic reactions take place.

The pyruvic acid created during glucoses can be guided into a complex series of energy-creating reactions, referred to as the Krebs cycle. This process also metabolizes fats into energy. The Krebs cycle accounts for 90 percent of the energy needed for training to compete in longer endurance races. This process is essential since the muscles contain instant energy in the form of A.T.P. which will be depleted within 10 to 15 seconds when exercising vigorously. After this period the oxygen must mix with A.T.P. in order to provide continuous energy.

When a person exercises vigorously, for more than 10 to 15 seconds, pyruvic acid is produced by way of glucoses at high rates. When pyruvic acid accumulates faster than the Krebs cycle is able to recycle it, lots of it has to wait in the bloodstream until it can be processed back to energy for additional glucoses. It is important to note that lactate should not be held responsible for either the burning sensation in the working muscles or the soreness, which often follows after a prolonged exercise period.

Once the exercise is complete, lactic acid depletes in a few minutes. Developing the ability to convert lactate will help the athlete run faster for a longer period of time.

Developing the process by which lactate is filtered into muscle cells is commonly referred to as the lactate shuttle. The lactate shuttle reveals that lactate is not just a byproduct of glucoses but is a high-octane fuel, helping the muscle cells meet their immediate energy requirements and store excess energy for future use.

The velocity of running that causes lactate to build up faster than it can be processed back to pyruvic is called the lactate threshold running velocity (LTRV). The velocity at which this action occurs is a measure of the amount of oxygen the athlete processes to muscle cells, as well as the level of efficiency of the mitochondria to convert pyruvic to energy. Mitochondria are minute motor units within each muscle cell, where aerobic energy is produced with the help of aerobic enzymes. If a person's LTRV is reached at a low level of speed, it simply means that the oxidative energy system in that individual's muscles is not very efficient. A key goal of training should be to progressively raise the athlete's LTRV to higher speeds. Beginning runners must systematically develop and improve their glycogenic system and lactate shuttle system concurrently. In that regard, emphasizing work that promotes lactate-shuttle efficiency will greatly enhance the advancement of the glucoses process. When a person runs, the feeling of discomfort is a result of running faster than their current LTRV, more so than that of a poor $\dot{V}O_2max$.

Improving the lactate shuttle system should receive a high priority in an athlete's efforts to train to race in endurance events. From day one, a key goal of an individual's training to race endurance events should be to progressively move their LTRV to higher and higher speeds. Doing so will mean that an athlete's operative energy system is improving and that their muscles are getting better at pulling lactate out of the blood and converting it to energy.

The ability of the muscles to snatch lactate from the blood depends on a protein (MCT) conversion. This protein is found on the outer edges of muscle membrane and can help transport lactate from the blood into the interior of the muscle cells. The greater the level of MCT concentrations in the blood, the faster the body can convert lactate into energy. In turn, the athlete will have a higher level of LTRV.

Scientific research reveals that to improve LTRV, fairly intense training is better than higher volumes of moderate intensity training. In fact, running at higher velocities can improve LTRV as much as 20 percent over the course of 4-to-6 months. It also improves the concentration of a key mitochondrial enzyme in the body called cytochromes. Cytochrome is a critically important oxidative enzyme found within the mitochondria and is linked to cap swings on LTRV. High-intensity workouts involving fairly heavy doses of sprint work, will improve LTRV.

CHAPTER 10
Optimal Training

The reason for an athlete's inability to maintain a specific pace during a workout or race is not due to the lack of oxygen available for glycolysis. Rather, it is the result of the lactate shuttle process not being able to keep up with the conversion of that lactate as quickly as it is produced by the specific rate of glycolysis. This factor puts workouts that improve lactate tolerance as a top training priority.

Figure 10-1 illustrates the optimal sequence of work for producing a complete runner, a progression that entails five elements: Gold Medal running form; functional strength; speed development; lactate conversion; and endurance.

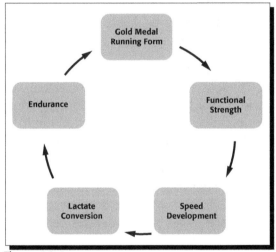

Figure 10-1

Gold medal running form is facilitated by performing skill drills that promote a tall, upright posture, with the trunk and head held directly over the hips, relaxed shoulders and arms, a quick turnover, and foot strike with a medium stride length. These drills can be combined with short runs of 30-to-150 meters at a fast, relaxed effort that will quickly buildup lactate faster than it can be converted back to energy.

Working on gold medal running form, as well as building lactate tolerance, enhances basic speed. Furthermore, adding short sprints of 30-to-60 meters to the aforementioned workout, will improve a runner's level of speed. At that point, including uphill and downhill running, spring running, and ballistic movements to the mix will help ensure that the runner is on the way to enhancing their basic speed. As detailed previously, basic speed is the single most important physiological variable in determining how fast a race can be run at any distance. Speed work can also enhance an athlete's overall endurance by helping to improve their $\dot{V}O_2$max.

In addition, speed work contributes to two key adaptations in the body—a reduced rate at which glycogen is burned and a reduction in the buildup of lactate during strenuous effort. Research shows that a decrease in the rate glycogen is burned during running promotes stamina, because more glycogen fuel remains in the tank to be utilized after any specific duration of effort. A more diminished buildup of lactate can indicate that lactate is being used efficiently for energy and that it is being broken down, instead of accumulating in the muscles.

One minute of sprint interval training has been found to achieve the same benefit as 42 minutes of running at 65 percent $\dot{V}O_2$max. Increasing the functional strength of the working muscles not only makes them stronger, it also makes them more resistant to fatigue. Activities for functional leg muscle strength can be incorporated into the warm-up and cool-down phases of a training session. Endurance development begins with any activity that causes the heart to accelerate its beating rhythm. This objective is undertaken mainly through running workouts. The more intense the workout, the greater its effect on aerobic development.

In order to run, force is created to produce forward movement. The source of this force is the human foot. The foot is a lever that does the actual work of running. The foot is made up of a heel bone, to which are attached tendons, ligaments, and soft tissue that make the front part flexible and resilient. The front part of the foot has elastic properties that allow it to stretch, and then snap quickly back to its original configuration contour.

The greater the force applied as the foot strikes the running surface, the quicker it can stretch and rebound. Running speed is directly related to how quickly the foot can get on and off the running surface. In order for the foot to create the greatest force, it must strike the running surface as far back under the center of the body as possible and with a downward thrust.

When the downward thrust is faster than the center of mass is moving forward, the runner can accelerate or maintain a specific running velocity. When the backward thrust of the foot slows to a velocity that is not compatible with that of the forward movement of the runner's body, the velocity will decrease. The shorter the race, the closer the runner comes to maintaining top speed. As the distance of the race increases, the lower the percentage of top speed that can be held in the race's entirety.

The faster a person's basic speed, the greater potential for racing any distance. The average velocity that can be maintained at any specific distance is referred to as an individual's speed endurance index. As such, running speed, can be broken down into the following categories: acceleration, which is up to 40 meters; true speed, which covers the distance from 40 meters to 80 meters; average basic performance speed, which is an individual's running velocity at 400 meters; and endurance velocity, which is a person's running velocity for 300 meters.

It is important to remember that athletes must also train their brain when working out. In that regard, engaging in race-specific training is recommended. While running at less-than-optimal speeds may improve an individual's $\dot{V}O_2$max, it may also reduce their running economy, as well as result in them developing a slow turnover with overstriding and heel strike.

An example of a proven lactate tolerance workout would include the following:

- 3 minutes at v$\dot{V}O_2$max
- 3-minute rest
- 1k at v$\dot{V}O_2$max
- Rest
- Intervals: 800-600-400-200
- Lead up LT: 50 meters fast, 50 easy, 100 meters fast, 100 easy, 150 fast, 150 easy; Perform as many as possible, advance to 200, 250 and 300.

CHAPTER 11 ———————————
The Beginner

Anyone, regardless of age or stature, who for whatever reason decides to run, has to start sometime, somewhere. Young children run spontaneously as part of their growth and development. Their running is characteristically carried out with free, unrestricted movements. Older youth and high school-age children mostly start a running program with a club or high school cross-country team. In reality, a number of people take up running when they are in their 30s or older.

Running is a natural movement that is viewed by most beginning runners as simply putting one foot in front of the other and then letting gravity do the rest. Beginning runners can be likened to a person who picks up a golf club and attempts to strike a ball for the first time. In both instances, the actions are mostly awkward because no previous neuromuscular patterns have been established to perform the act correctly.

A person who wants to learn how to play golf can enlist the services of a professional teacher for assistance. Youth, high school, and collegiate runners typically are under the guidance of a coach who is in charge of their training. In contrast, late-comers to running generally do not seek professional help to assist them with their running program. As a result, they establish their own version of how to run.

Beginning runners, those with some previous experience and those who are well trained, all have the same needs when it comes to developing their potential to race. Poor running posture, overstriding, and slow foot and arm movements are typical of the entry-level runner.

In general, many coaches fail to see the importance of teaching novice runners to be able to relax their upper bodies and arms and to place their foot strike so that excessive energy is not wasted during the act of running. The first-time runner, the runner returning from a period of rest, or the runner coming off a base-building session can prepare for a competitive season by designing a training program around how to run correctly.

One Step at a Time

Running is accomplished by moving forward one step at a time, using a springy action made possible by the elastic springs in an individual's feet and legs. Energy is stored during each foot strike and released at toe-off, making the act of running energy efficient. To become an accomplished runner, an individual must move forward with a coordinated combination of stride length and stride frequency of the lower limbs, with balance and stabilization help from the upper limbs and core.

As noted previously, the neural system is in command of all muscular actions that are involved in running. An inability by the neural system to maintain balance limits the capacity for optimum stride length, especially when running at mid-to-maximum running velocities, i.e., $\dot{V}O_2max$ running velocities. Sensor input from the central nervous system will, in effect, regulate stride length and stride frequency.

During an endurance race the body continues to struggle for balance and stability. When the center of mass passes over the support limb, the body must maintain dynamic equilibrium, i.e., a tall erect torso, with the head, shoulders, and hips in a line directly over the collapsed support foot. The perfect model for demonstrating this position is Haile Gebrselassie.

As an endurance runner becomes more efficient through training, running economy improves. Through running, the body develops its own combination of stride length and frequency in its effort to achieve a desired velocity.

As noted previously, retired Olympic athlete, Dr. Ralph Mann has shown through high-speed motion analysis studies that too much time in the air and too much time on the ground hinder velocity movement. He also found that reducing foot contact time by as little as 1/100 seconds produces marked improvement in races of any distance, mainly because reducing foot strike time improves stride rate (turnover).

In reality, foot strike tie, turnover, and heel cycle determine race times. A lack of functional running strength to maintain a rhythmical stride length that is compatible with the desired turnover leads to overstriding and the inefficient use of energy.

Positioning the trunk to achieve balance, correct arm action, and foot strike are learned through running-skill drills and running-specific strength activities. Improving maximal aerobic power is of utmost importance in the development of an athlete's ability to race in endurance events. Running alone, however, will not develop maximal neuromuscular power.

American coaches and athletes need to understand that running is first and foremost a neural thing and that coaching the neuromuscular system can no longer be ignored. They must come to the understanding that aerobic power and neuromuscular power must be developed concurrently, not separately or singularly.

The neural system coordinates muscular contractions. Scientific research indicates that the athlete who wants to run more quickly must teach the nervous system not only to stimulate the muscles that create greater force in a shorter period of time, but also to improve the manner in which the nervous system integrates muscular activity.

Muscles that create propulsive force must be stimulated at just the right time, just as muscles that might restrict movement must be relaxed at the proper moment. Muscles will not automatically accomplish this step on their own and must be coached to respond to the commands of the nervous system. Running mile after mile at moderate velocities is not neural training. In fact, it is a detriment to fast running, because it does not promote the ability of the nervous system to generate high muscular force. As a result, it retards basic genetic speed.

Neural training features quick, forceful movements and places a high premium on coordinating muscular activity in the most efficient manner possible. Quick forceful contractions are desirable for endurance runners if they expect to reach their optimal race performance.

To paraphrase the Bible, the body cannot exist on bread alone. There has to be some grape juice flowing through the veins. In other words, an individual cannot become a complete runner through running alone. Athletes have to supplement their aerobic power development with dynamic warm-ups and circuit training that collectively promote functional leg strength and quick-foot strikes. In fact, as noted previously, if coaches would allot 30 percent of their squad's practice time to developing the neuromuscular aspects of running, they would be totally amazed at the improvement in race performance. Such a schedule would still allow 70 percent of an athlete's workout time to the development of aerobic power.

Coaches need to stop thinking about a mileage quota and let the number of miles run per week be a result of carefully planned workouts that are dedicated to developing the complete runner. Somewhat inexplicably, coaches at all competitive levels continue to persist on developing an aerobic base through a buildup of mileage before adding elements that form a base that addresses the other physiological variables of endurance training. The primary problem with this line of thinking is that by the time an aerobic base is accomplished, it is too late in the season to efficiently establish a base for speed, fatigue-resistant muscle strengthening, and other variables of training.

The other issue with developing an aerobic base before any other variable theory is that while running mega miles at a moderate velocity, the athletes, left to their own means, almost without exception develop a slow foot strike, which promotes overstriding. This outcome leads to a heel-first touchdown and a braking action with every step. As a rule, during the process of developing an aerobic base, neuromuscular patterns that are detrimental to speed development are firmly established in the central nervous system, which cannot be changed significantly during the period of speed training.

Coaches who are successful at the regional, state, and national level argue that aerobic base first and a mileage quota works for them, so why change? They fail to consider the fact that everyone else is using the same training scheme and that they tend to be more successful simply because of their ability to accumulate greater numbers of athletes and motivate them to work harder than other coaches are able to do.

In essence, it is the coach's personality and ability to recruit athletes to the program and then motivate them to work that typically makes for a successful program. Coaches who can attract large numbers of athletes to the program are highly successful, because the more bodies that are training, the better the percentage for finding athletes who are genetically gifted enough to perform well. It is highly unlikely that any coach at the youth, high school, or collegiate level has the development of an Olympic-caliber athlete as their major coaching goal. It is, however, through these ranks that such athletes emerge.

Unfortunately, when American elite endurance runners compete against other nation's elite athletes they find themselves woefully unprepared to answer the surges during a race and the finishing kicks at the end. The reason that the elite runners of the United States cannot match the speed of other international athletes is that no one ever taught them how to run fast.

American coaches at all levels are so consumed with developing cardio power that they virtually ignore the importance of neuromuscular power. As such, they do not give the development of a base for speed its proper status for racing in endurance events.

Many coaches are very traditional. They coach the way that they were coached or trained. More often than not, they ignore the scientific research that is available that points out the importance of speed development, fatigue-resistant functional muscle strength, and the fundamentals of running technique.

Proper Running Mechanics

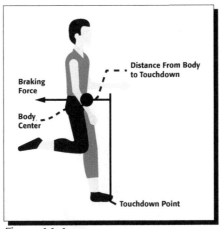

Figure 11-1

Proper form for running entails having a tall upright torso, with the head and shoulders directly over the hips. The foot that provides the power should land as far back under the center of mass as possible. The recovery leg should be flexed, with the heel higher than the knee and poised to drive forward. The arms should be bent to approximately 90 degrees. All of the muscles in the shoulders and lower arms should be completely relaxed (Figure 11-2).

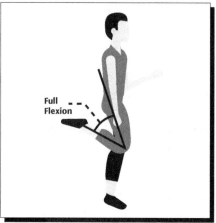

Figure 11-2

How the runner places the power foot when running is very important, given that it serves as the lever that provides the power to propel the body forward. The action of the foot is a striking motion as it is traveling downward to make contact with the running surface. This technique is the beginning of backside mechanics.

The foot should first make contact with the running surface on its flexible part. The contour of the foot causes it to hit slightly on the outside (pronation), and then, as the foot collapses, it rotates slightly to the inside (supination), before leaving the surface from the large toes. This outsideinside action causes the foot to literally screw itself into the surface, exerting forceful thrust for forward motions. As the foot leaves the surface with a final backward push of the big toes, the backside mechanics are initiated (Figure 11-3).

Figure 11-3

As noted in Chapter 6, in order to run fast, the athlete must maximize both the leg recovery and the touchdown rotation speed. Of all the upper-leg actions, upper-leg speed at touchdown is the most critical factor, since it affects the amount of forward braking, as well as the amount of ground contact time (Figure 11-4). The athlete must minimize the lower-leg angle, during both the recovery and as the ankle crosses over the support leg. A detailed review of what runners can do to enhance their ability to run fast is addressed in Chapter 6.

Figure 11-4

❏ *Improving Stride Length*

Turnover is also a critical factor in efficient, effective running. The key to this phase of running is to shorten the amount of time that the foot stays on the surface at touchdown.

Aging and Endurance Running

How does aging effect endurance running? Research indicates that endurance athletes begin to slow in their late 30s and declines more as they age. Generally, individuals can expect a reduction of 0.5 percent to 1.0 percent per year in the level of their $\dot{V}O_2max$ from ages 35 to 60. From 30 to 70 years up to 40 percent of a person's $\dot{V}O_2max$ is lost, primarily because their maximal heart rate declines at the rate of one beat per year. At about age 40, individuals start to lose muscle tissue. In addition, the ability of their body to synthesize protein is reduced. Furthermore, type II muscle fiber composition decreases after age 50. The size of type I muscles also decreases. As a result, a person's level of strength and endurance is reduced.

❏ *The Ancient Road Warrior*

Just because an individual is 40, 50, and 60+ does not mean that they cannot run fast. While aging has an effect on stride length and running power, runners can conserve both for longer periods of time than a person might think. In fact, it is the disuse of muscles that are specific to running that erodes performance, more so than the aging process. If runners can develop a turnover of at least 96 (192 steps) per minute, they will experience minimal decline in stride rate, even at age 55.

In essence, individuals slow with age because of a loss of power, a decreased level of functional leg strength, and a diminished range of motion that causes their stride length to shorten. Mostly, however, they digress in performance with age because their neuromuscular system has not been motivated properly to maintain muscle consistency.

Most individuals begin to lose muscle strength and $\dot{V}O_2$max once they reach the age of 40. They can slow the effects of aging, however, by engaging in activities that stimulate their neuromuscular system to produce the quicker and more forceful actions. Running-skill drills, functional muscle strengthening, and speed-enhancing activities have been shown to slow the process of aging, as it effects racing in endurance event. Without question, no one has found the fountain of youth, or is likely to do so. The human body, as science reaffirms, is a fairly open book. All muscle cells thrive on the stress-and-adaptation phenomenon. As such, to a point, aging runners can mitigate much of the decline in their physiological capabilities, by continuing to stress the systems of their bodies through targeted training.

All of the cells that comprise the organs and muscles that are involved in the physiology of running are muscle cells. When muscles contract to cause movement, the heart speeds up its rate of beating in its effort to send oxygen rich blood to the muscles doing the work of running. During this effort, stress is increased in the body's cardio pulmonary system.

The adaptation of muscle cells to the stress level that is applied results in an increase of strength that is proportional to the stress. In other words, training to run fast for long period periods of time involves a systematic increase in stress that allows muscle cells to adapt during rest, a process that also applies to aging runners.

❑ *The Good News*

The decline in muscle power that occurs as people age can be retarded by putting more emphasis on stimulating the central nervous system to cause muscles to react with quick and forceful actions that can be carried out over a designated period of time. In fact, an individual's lactate threshold may actually increase, compared to their $\dot{V}O_2$max. Among the steps that can help individuals continue to race at a relatively high level as they grow older include the following:
- Reduce their mileage and increase the percentage of quality of their workouts.
- Spend an appropriate amount of time performing functional strength training.
- Work on improving their flexibility.
- Give special attention to strengthening their core, hamstring, and glute muscles.
- Increase the amount of cross-training activities, e.g., biking, swimming, and rowing, they do.

- Develop a quicker turnover to compensate for a reduction in their stride length.
- Develop more power for each foot strike.
- Expand the amount of hill running they do and work on their gold medal running form.
- Add circuit training to their weekly workout scheme.
- Perform functional-strengthening to promote fatigue-resistant muscle tissue.

Adolescents and Endurance Running

Runners in the throes of puberty have superpowers—literally. A British study compared 12 boys and 13 men doing 10 sets of 10-second sprints. The boys sustained their power output better than the men, partly because teens regenerate creatine (a compound that supplies muscles with energy) more quickly than older runners. Furthermore, levels of lactate, the by-product that accompanies intense efforts, are naturally lower in teens.

Girls share the same ability to pour on the power. In fact, they can sustain it even better than boys. Japanese researchers found that in a series of sprints, teenage girls lost 10 percent less power than boys of their age did. That being said, as muscle mass piles on, boys have a distinct upper hand. "Boys develop proportionally more muscle mass than girls do and get the natural power advantage," says Cameron Blimkie, Ph.D., professor of kinesiology at McMaster University in Ontario.

Running also offers another distinct benefit for adolescents. For example, as adolescents develop over the course of their maturation (physical growth) process, running, as well as other weight-bearing exercises, helps make their bones as dense as possible. In fact, research shows that most young runners tend to have a higher level of bone health, when compared to their non-running adolescent counterparts.

CHAPTER 12 ━━━━━━━━━━━━━━━

Workouts

Coordinating running workouts with neuromuscular development should be a priority the first day of practice. The underlying focus of the effort should be on strength development and speed enhancement. Initially, the workouts should begin with a general strengthening period covering the first four weeks of training. This training phase is where a base for running efficiency, speed, lactate conversion, and the efficient development of endurance is commenced. The following guidelines for planning a training season to develop the complete runner are recommended:

- Begin every workout with a dynamic warm-up that features running skills and functional-muscle strengthening activities. End each session with a dynamic cool-down. Schedule the athletes for 120 minutes of their time. At the beginning of the season, the warm-up may last up to 45 minutes, because the running skills and strengthening activities must be taught and the athletes must learn to perform them correctly. This schedule allows 45 minutes for running and conditioning, as well as time time for the dynamic cool-down and extra strength work. The warm-up, which must completely prepare the muscles for fast running, is considered a "mini" workout itself. As the season progresses, the time spent with the warm-up phase can be reduced. Subsequently, the tempo of each activity can be increased.

- Use short segments of running, while working on a quick foot strike and turnover. Use the short reps to learn how to relax, while running with a tall and relaxed posture. Learn to run smooth, fast, and relaxed. Adherence to the proper mechanics involved in running skills must be reinforced every day.

- Initiate high levels of lactate for numerous short periods, and utilize circuit training as the basis for working on lactate-threshold running economy and improving overall body strength.

- Work on speed enhancement daily; incorporate speed-development drills into the workout.

- Begin building an endurance base and enhancing $\dot{V}O_2max$ by using Fartlek and circuit workouts.

- Gradually increase the length of runs, using steady-state runs with quality segments Check turnover frequently. The running conditioning phase of the daily work session must cover all the physiological variables of endurance running over a 21-day period, not just $\dot{V}O_2max$ improvement. Speed enhancement and lactate conversion should also be addressed.

- After the first five weeks of training, give the six-minute run test to determine each athlete's $v\dot{V}O_2max$ and $\dot{V}O_2max$ fitness level. Calculate each athlete's training pace for goal-pace interval work. Use $v\dot{V}O_2max$ (variable) paces for interval work to improve maximum oxygen uptake. As race performances improve, upgrade the paces for the interval work, using segments at·800m, 1500m, 3k, 5k, and 10k effort. Employ multi-tiered training paces, and train at race-goal paces that are both faster and slower than the runner's preferred race distance.

- Design daily workouts to accomplish a specific training goal, and let the mileage run be the result of a carefully planned workout, as opposed to a set mileage quota.
- End the workout with a cool-down. After a period of exertion, the muscles need to return to their normal state and begin a period of recovery. The cool-down is the last phase of the workout and consists of easy running and functional muscle strengthening activities. Additional strength work can be added to the cool-down two or three days per week as practical. Recovery days can be best used for cross training, functional muscle strengthening and running skill drills.

Why Do Individuals Run?

The simple and most basic answer is because they can. Even with all of the modern modes of transportation, walking and running are the major means by which individuals move their bodies from place to place. Humans are runners basically, because of an inherent need over the centuries to find food and shelter to survive.

The foot has evolved into a powerful and efficient lever, providing the force for forward movement. All aerobic, anaerobic, and neuromuscular power that humans create culminates with the foot striking a surface. The brain and central nervous system control how fast and how far individuals move.

Millions of people have an inherent desire to test themselves with competitive racing. Racing other humans is also a means by which a person tests their fitness level. A person's fitness level is a measure of the relative strength of all of the physiological variables involved in racing endurance events. As such, when training to race in endurance events, individuals need to stress all of these variables concurrently, as opposed to developing one before addressing another one. Furthermore, running is an outpouring, a release from tension. As such, collectively, the inherent reasons for running will continue to drive people to engage in the activity as long as there are humans.

In order for a person to run, two basic phenomena must occur. First, the brain signals the working muscles to contract and relax in a coordinated effort, causing the movement at the joints. Second, the heart immediately reacts by sending oxygen-rich blood to the muscles doing the work.

Since muscle contraction cannot occur without oxygen to mix with stored glycogen, running is initially a neurological event. Various muscles and organs subsequently become involved in keeping the process of running continuing over a period of time. The whole body then adapts to the continued stress of strength development. Since running is both a neurological and a cardiopulmonary phenomenon, it is imperative that efforts to strengthen both of these systems are included in the training scheme for runners, as opposed to concentrating solely on the athlete's cardiopulmonary system.

All movements in sporting events are controlled by the central nervous system. The neural system consists of the brain, spinal cord, muscle cells, and neurons that control the contraction and relaxation of the muscle fibers. Every movement begins with a concept in the brain. The brain sends signals to activate the muscle fibers involved in the movement to be performed.

The neural muscular system is best developed through a series of dynamic activities that feature not only the runner's body weight as the resistance, as well as dynamic movements that enhance running rhythm with quick on-and-off-the-running-surface foot action. Incorporating neuromuscular enhancement activities into daily warm-up and cool-down sessions is a very effective way of incorporating them into a training scheme. Performing neural muscular activities, alternated with $\dot{V}O_2$max-pace running for 70-to-80 seconds in a circuit-type session, is also an excellent way to integrate neuromuscular activities into an individual's training regimen.

The neuromuscular aspects of running are key components in racing any distance. Neural training should focus on three essential factors: strengthen the muscles that do the work of running through dynamic movements that are specific to the act of running; develop a running economy model that emulates elite runners who have the best running form; and develop a turnover relative to the time and distance of the event to be raced with a quick on-and-off-the-running-surface foot strike.

The two major determinantes for developing neuromuscular power are running skills and functional muscle strengthening. With proper coaching in these areas, an endurance runner can improve their basic performance speed. Basic performance speed is the single most important physiological variable in determining how fast someone can race at any distance.

With correct frontside and backside running mechanics, an athlete can position their feet to strike the running surface as far back under the center of mass as possible, causing a quick on-and-off-the-surface foot strike, while keeping a turnover at 98 per minute. Quick feet are as important in the 5k as they are in the 100 meters. An endurance runner, whose muscles are capable of fast-force production with rapid, well-coordinated explosive contractions, has a definite edge in racing, given that racing velocity is inversely proportionate to foot-strike time. The less time the foot is in contact with the surface, the faster the race time.

In most instances, the muscles of a beginning runner—those that do the work of running—are not strong enough to absorb the impact of gravity coming with each contact with a running surface. These muscles have not been strengthened concurrently with the increase in intensity and volume of work.

Coaches, however, can coordinate the workload of their athletes to ensure that adequate attention is given to improving muscle strength through functional muscle strengthening. Functional muscle strengthening involves performing resistance activities that are specific to the act of running. Functional strengthening of the muscles that do the work of running will enable them to become more fatigue-resistant. It will also greatly improve speed endurance.

Functional muscle training not only strengthens the muscle fibers, it also teaches the neuromuscular system to coordinate muscle-fiber contractions with those muscles that are not contracting, thus preventing muscle tears and promoting greater agility. Since muscles do the work involved in running, it is to the athlete's advantage to make them as strong as possible. In that regard, in order to strengthen the muscles, tendons, and ligaments that are involved in undertaking the work of running, athletes need to perform functional activities.

The cardiopulmonary system includes the heart, lungs and capillaries. The cardiopulmonary system is best strengthened by exposing it to training that entails a multi-tiered level of running intensities for specific periods of time. When these various intensities are rotated through a training cycle, endurance, lactate tolerance, $\dot{V}O_2max$, and speed endurance are all enhanced concurrently.

Such a system of training has several objectives, including improve the strength of the heart muscle; improve the stroke volume of the heart; develop as many capillaries as possible around the muscle fibers; improve the size and number of mitochondria in each cell; and improve the body's ability to change the work products of glycolysis to useful fuel. Possessing a high $\dot{V}O_2max$ and lactate threshold running velocity are not enough to produce the complete runner. These physiological assets must be complemented by total neuromuscular development, if a runner expects to hold race pace, cover surges and be able to respond to the finishing kick of other runners. In fact, as noted previously, creating neuromuscular power is as important to racing in events of 800 meters to 1,000 meters as is developing cardiovascular power.

CHAPTER 13 ━━━━━━━━━━━━━━━
Warm-Up and Cool-Down Exercises

The Warm-Up

The warm-up should involve more than just raising the temperature in the muscles by increasing circulation. The warm-up must completely prepare all of the muscle groups to do a quality workout. In fact, everything that individuals do in their workouts, including the warm-up and cool-down, should be specific to training the physiological variables involved in improving a person's fitness level and the ability to compete.

The warm-up, which should be dynamic and recruit all types of muscle fibers, can be a mini-workout in itself. Warm-ups can last up to 30 minutes in the early season and be reduced as the season progresses, e.g., to 15 minutes. A sample warm-up can include the following steps:

- Start the warm-up with a 10-minute progression of performing running skills.
- Begin by quickstep-walking, with ankle-over-ankle action, while maintaining good posture and proper arm action.
- Perform this action for 10 seconds x 6 and then progress to quickstep ankle-over-ankle running action for 10 seconds.
- Next, perform ankle-over-knee running action for 30 seconds.
- Continue this sequence for 10 minutes and then proceed to the dynamic skills and strengthening phase of the warm-up.
- Perform these activities in a tall posture, with the head and shoulders directly on his hips. Emphasize the correct execution of mechanics, while performing these activities.
- Begin with slow, deliberate action and progress to faster movement.

The Cool-Down

The cool-down (also referred to as a warm-down) is a period of performing less-demanding exercises following a workout that is designed to allow the body to return, gradually, to its normal physiological level. Among the benefits of a cool-down are the fact that it helps bring the exerciser's heart rate and breathing patterns back to normal; it helps prepare the muscles for the next bout of exercise; and it helps remove waste products in the body (such as lactic acid) that can build up after rigorous activity. While most of these products will ultimately dissipate in the body on their own, the cool-down facilitates the process. A sample cool-down can entail the following steps:

- Begin the cool-down with five minutes of easy quickstep running, while staying completely relaxed.
- Perform a series of strides and do functional strength activities.

Among the basic factors to consider when performing functional strengthening activities are the following:

- Maintain a good running posture, with the head and shoulders directly above the hips.
- Stay relaxed and look straight ahead.
- Once an exercise is completed, move directly to the next.
- Learn to perform each exercise correctly and then work towards moving more quickly. Form should never be sacrificed for more speed.
- When performing any activity that involves absorbing the exerciser's body weight, do so on a forgiving surface, such as grass, dirt, or mats.

Sample Warm-Ups and Cool-Downs

Warm-up activities should initially involve doing 10 reps and then advanced to performing 30 seconds of a continuous repetition. It is important that athletes do not stretch to warm-up, but rather warm-up to stretch. The following warm-ups and cool-downs are examples of selected routines that were employed in various venues, including past Olympic sites. The list also includes three sample active stretch warm-up routines.

❑ *Warm-Up: Atlanta*

1. Running progression (10 minutes)
2. Body squats (10 reps)
3. Bench step ups (10 reps on each leg)
4. Bench dips (10 reps)
5. Bench squats (10 reps on each leg)
6. Feet up push-up (10 reps)
7. Vertical hops—10 quick hops, using the flexible part of the foot with a 3-inch rise (10 reps on each leg)
8. Rhythm V-hops (8" x 10 each leg, 8" x 10 each leg, 3" x 10 each leg)
9. Leg swings, bicycle, and hip flexor (10 each leg)
10. Speed, agility ladder, walk, run (2 in – 2 out, 6 each)
11. Running progression (10 minutes)
12. Acceleration ladder (x 6 40m)

❑ *Warm-Up: Beijing*

1. Running progression (10 minutes)
2. Hip flexor leg swings (15 each leg)

3. Hamstring leg swings (15 each leg)
4. Quickstep walk—step one ankle over the other (30m x 2)
5. Quickstep skip (30m x 2)
6. Hamstring skip (30m x 2)
7. Squat jump (30m x 2)
8. Double leg hops (30m x 2)
9. Scissor hops (30m x 2)
10. Single leg hops (30m x 2 each leg, quick)
11. Single leg hops (30m x 2 for distance)
12. Spring running (50m x 2)
13. Three knee up sprint (20m x 2)
14. Run 18 turnovers (10 sec x 6 - mile effort)

❑ *Warm-Up: London*

1. Easy quick stop (10 minute run)
2. Bodyweight squats (10 reps)
3. Forward lunges (10 reps each leg)
4. Squat hops (20m x 2)
5. Scissor hop (20m x 2)
6. Quick hops (20 x 2 each leg)
7. Leg swings hamstring and hip flexor (10 reps each leg)
8. Speed acceleration ladder (x 6 40m)
9. Running progression (10 minutes)
10. Acceleration ladder (x 6 40m)
11. Run 18 turnovers (in 10 sec x 2)
12. Accelerations (30m)

❑ *Warm-Up: Tokyo*

1. Running progression (10 minutes)
2. Leg swings—hamstrings and hip flexor (15 each leg)
3. Quickstep skip (30m x 2)
4. Quickstep walk (30m x 2)
5. Quickstep run (30m x 2)
6. Bench step up (10 each leg)
7. Bench push-up (15)
8. Bench squats (10)
9. Bench dips (15)
10. Run in place with high heel follow through (15 sec buildup x 2)

11. Run 18 turnovers (in 10 sec x 2)
12. Run 36 turnovers (in 10 sec x 2)
13. Run 54 turnovers (in 10 sec x 2)

❏ *Cool-Down: Tokyo*

1. Quickstep run (10 minutes at an easy pace)
2. Strides (3 forward, 3 backward—barefoot, if possible x 6)
3. Crazy feet (barefoot if possible) (5 minutes)
4. Core—front/side/back plank (15 sec each x 2)
5. Stretch IT band, hamstrings, and quads (30 sec each x 3)

❏ *Warm-Up: Munich*

1. Running progression (10 minutes)
2. Feet up squats (15 each leg)
3. Feet up push-ups (15)
4. Step ups (15)
5. Bench dips (15)
6. V-hops (15 each leg)
7. Squat jumps (10 x 2)
8. Burpies (5)
9. Quickstep run ankle over ankle (20m x 2)
10. Quickstep run step ankle over calf (20m x 2)

❏ *Cool-Down: Los Angeles*

1. 6 x 100m strides—3 forward, 3 backward (6x)
2. Eccentric reaches—center/right/left (15 each position)
3. Crazy feet (30m each position x 2)
4. Stretch IT band, hamstrings, and quads (30 sec each x 3)

❏ *Cool-Down: Seoul*

1. Strides—3 forward, 3 backward (6x)
2. Crazy feet (30m each position x 2)
3. Core—front/side/back plank (15 sec each x 2)
4. Stretch IT band, hamstrings, and quads (30 sec each x 3)

❑ *Warm-Up: Oregon*

1. Running progression (10 minutes)
2. Leg swings (hip flexor 20, hamstring 20)
3. Walking lunges (10 each leg x 2)
4. Squat jumps (10 x 2)
5. Scissor hops (10 x 2)
6. Quick vertical hops (4 inch in place, 30 each leg)
7. Single leg hops (30m x 2 speed and distance)
8. Quickstep skip (30m x 2)
9. Hamstring skip (30m x 2)
10. Quickstep walk (30m x 2 ankle over ankle, run in place on balls of feet, build up to ankle over knee)
11. Knee up sprint (3 quick knees to chest, sprint 10m x 4)

❑ *Cool-Down: Oregon*

1. Quickstep run (10 minutes easy)
2. Strides—3 forward, 3 backward (6x)
3. Eccentric reaches—center/right/left (15 each position)
4. Runner's pose (15 each leg)
5. Crazy feet (30m each position x 2)
6. Stretch IT band, hamstrings, and quads (30 sec each x 3)

❑ *Warm-Up: Escalon*

1. Running progression (10 minutes)
2. Bench push-ups (15)
3. Bench step ups (15 each leg)
4. Bench dips (25)
5. Bench half squats (hold 11th 10 sec each leg, x 10)
6. Hamstring leg swings, bicycle (10 each leg)
7. Hamstring leg swings reverse bicycle (10 each leg)
8. Walking lunges (30m)
9. Squat hops (30m)
10. Quick skips (30m)
11. Power skips (30m)
12. Speed agility ladders quick feet (x 6)
13. Acceleration ladders (x 6 40m)

❑ *Cool-Down: Escalon*

1. Quickstep run (5 minutes, easy)
2. 100 strides (3 forward, 3 backward, x6)
3. Crazy feet, walk on toes straight out (20m x 2)
4. Walk on heels, toes straight out (200m x 2)
5. Repeat 3, while running, skipping bunny hops (30m x 2)
6. Core—front/side/back plank (15 sec each x 2)
7. Stretch IT band, hamstrings, and quads (30 sec each x 3)

❑ *Active Stretch Warm-Up #1*

1. Running progression (10 minutes)
2. Leg swings hamstrings and hip flexor (10 each leg)
3. Forward single leg lunges (10 each leg)
4. Side single leg lunges (10 each leg)
5. Squat hops (10)
6. Scissor hops (30m x 2)
7. Five-count burpies (8)
8. Box stepups (10 each leg)
9. Box bench dips (10)
10. Box squats (10)
11. Box push-ups (10)
12. Single leg hops 4″ vertical rises (10 each leg)
13. Ladders (x 6 40m)
14. Accelerations (20m knee-up, toe-up x 2)

❑ *Active Stretch Warm-Up #2*

1. Quickstep runs (10 minutes, easy)
2. Standing squats (10)
3. Single leg forward lunges (10 each leg)
4. Side lunges (10 each leg)
5. Squat hops (10)
6. Scissor hops (20m x 2)
7. Five-count burpies (8)
8. Box step-ups (10 each leg)
9. Bench dips (10 slowly)
10. Toe-up squats (10 each leg)

11. Feet-up push-up (10 slowly)
12. Quick vertical hops (10 each leg)
13. Speed agility ladders (x 6 40m)
14. Acceleration ladder (x 6 40m)
15. Accelerations (20m knee-up, toe-up x 2)

❑ *Active Stretch Warm-Up #3*

1. Quickstep run (10 minutes, easy)
2. Body squats (15)
3. Forward lunges (15)
4. Side lunges (15)
5. Walking lunges (20m x 2)
6. Squat hops (20m x 2)
7. Scissor hops (30m x 2)
8. Power skip (30m x 2)
9. Rhythm hops (4" x 15 each leg, 8" x 15 each leg)
10. Leg swings—hip flexor and hamstring (20 each leg)

❑ *Running-Specific Warm-up*

The ultimate limitations in any race performance lie within the neuromuscular system, not the cardiovascular system. The brain is the neural governor of exercise intensity. Muscles will respond to training with a very high intensity, leading to a greater willingness to tolerate very strenuous efforts. Running is a closed-circuit activity, which can be enhanced by performing the following warm-up activities:

1. Quickstep run (10 minutes, easy)
2. Walk on toes straight ahead, in and out (30m x 2)
3. Walk on heels straight ahead, in and out (30m x 2)
4. Quickstep skip (30m x 2)
5. Spring running (50m x 2)
6. V-hops with dorsa flex 8" (15 each leg)
7. Rhythm hops (3" x 10 each leg, 8" x 10 each leg)
8. Run 18 turnovers, 10-second step, counting (in 6/30 sec recovery)
9. Easy 3 min then proceed to work out

❑ *Special Warm-Up for Workout Involving Intervals*

1. Running progression (10 minutes)
2. Walk on toes pointed straight ahead (2 x 30m)

3. Walk on toes pointed in (2 x 30m)
4. Walk on toes pointed out (2 x 30m)
5. Walk on heels, toes pointed straight ahead (2 x 30m)
6. Walk on heels, toes pointed in (2 x 30m)
7. Walk on heels, toes pointed out (2 x 30m)
8. Repeat 2, 3, and 4, while skipping
9. Repeat 2, 3, and 4, while quickstep lazy running
10. Repeat 2, 3, and 4, while walking on heels
11. Repeat 2, 3, and 4, while bunny hopping
12. Vertical in, quick hops (20 each leg)
13. 50m strides (2x)
14. Spring run (4x 50)
15. 100m strides—3 forward, 3 backward (6x)
16. Run easy for three minutes, and then proceed with workout. Warm-up is equal to 2.3 miles of running 25 percent quality.

❑ *Special Warm-Up #2*

1. Running progression (10 minutes)
2. Leg swings—hip flex hamstrings claw back (15 each leg)
3. Walk high on toes, feet straight ahead (20m x 2), toes out (20m x 2), toes in (20m x 2)
4. Repeat 3, while walking on heels
5. Repeat 3, while skipping on front part of foot
6. Spring running on midfoot (50m x 4 short springy strides)
7. Dorsa-flex bounces (10 quick 6")

❑ *Additional Strength Activities That Can Be Included in the Special Warm-up*

1. Pull up (5)
2. Pull up, knee-overs (5)
3. Bar dips (5)
4. Wheel on bar dip frame (15 seconds graduated)
5. Snatch lifts (1/3 body weight) (5 reps x 3)
6. Military press (10 each arm, start with 15 lb dumbbell)
7. Plyometric jumps (30m right-right-left/left-left-right x 3)
8. Eccentric stand-ups from a seated position (15)

CHAPTER 14 ━━━━━━━━━

The Nervous System of the Body: Understanding the Basics

The nervous system of the body is an integral factor in training athletes of all competitive interests, fitness levels, and movement skills. It is the part of the body that processes information (from both inside and outside the body) and then dispatches instructions to the rest of the body, thereby facilitating an appropriate response. As such, it is the part of the body that ultimately enables a runner to enhance their level of performance, for example, by reducing their foot strike time, improving their stride rate, and extending their stride length. In essence, it achieves such a lofty outcome when the brain undergoes certain complex processes in response to practicing or experiencing a specific skill that leads to the subsequent development of an improved level of either a defined ability or a particular performance-related aptitude.

How Does the Nervous System Work?

The nervous system is the body's software. To a large degree, it determines how the hardware of the body (i.e., muscles, bones, and joints) performs. In that regard, it has a very substantial impact on performance.

Understandably, the nervous system plays a critical role in how well an athlete performs. As such, it is the component of the body that coordinates the actions of the runner by rapidly and precisely transmitting signals to and from different parts of the body via neurons (i.e., nerve cells) that subsequently initiate movement.

At the cellular level, the nervous system is distinguished by the presence of these nerve cells. The human body contains a vast number of these neurons. The brain, for example, consists of about 100 billion neurons, while the spinal cord has over 13 million of them.

The nervous system is very quick. As such, it can transmit impulses up to 100 meters per second. Furthermore, messages can be conveyed to the brain as fast as 180 miles per hour.

What Are the Key Elements of the Nervous System?

- Basil ganglia: a vital group of clusters of neurons in the brain that are located deep beneath the cerebral cortex that controls all sorts of voluntary movement

- Brain: the central organ of the human nervous system; consists of the cerebrum, the brain stem, and the cerebellum; controls most of the activities of the body
- Central nervous system: Consisting of the brain and the spinal cord, a complex of nerve tissues that controls the activities of the body; sends signals from one cell to others, or from one body part to others; receives feedback
- Cerebellum: the part of the brain at the back of the skull, whose function is to coordinate and regulate muscular activity
- Extrafusal fibers: the standard muscle fibers of the skeleton that are innervated by alpha motor neurons and generate tension by contracting, thereby allowing for skeletal movement
- Golgi tendon organ: proprioceptive sensory receptor organ that senses changes in muscle tension; lies at the origins and intersections of muscle fibers into the tendons of skeletal muscle; helps prevent overstretching of tendons
- Intrafusal fibers: skeletal muscle fibers that function as specialized sensory organs in the body (proprioceptors) and detect the amount and rate of change in the length of a muscle; sensitive to both force and velocity of change
- Motor cortex: the part of the cerebral cortex in the brain where the nerve impulses originate that initiate voluntary muscular activity.
- Motor unit: consists of a motor neuron and the skeletal fibers that are innervated by that neuron's axonal terminals. Groups of motor units often work together to coordinate the contractions of a single muscle
- Nerves: cylindrical bundles of fibers that emanate from the brain and spinal cord, and branch repeatedly to innervate every part of the body
- Nervous system: consists of two components—central nervous system and the peripheral nervous system
- Peripheral nervous system: consists mainly of nerves that connect the central nervous system to every other part of the body
- Spinal cord: the cylindrical bundle of nerve fibers and associated tissue that is enclosed in the spine and connects nearly all parts of the body to the brain, with which it forms the central nervous system

What Is the Role of the Brain in Movement?

The brain is the command center for all human movement, including that of a runner. The area of the brain most involved in controlling voluntary movements is the motor cortex. To initiate purposeful movement, the motor cortex must first receive various pieces of information from the various lobes of the brain, e.g., the body's relative position in space (parietal lobe); the movement-related objective to be attained and an appropriate strategy for attaining it (frontal lobe); memories of past movement-related strategies (temporal lobe); etc.

In essence, movement is initiated when messages, which are originated in the cortex, are sent to the muscles. Before they reach the muscles, they are "filtered" at the basil ganglia, which selects which "instructions" are executed and which are inhibited. All of this happens very, very quickly.

As this book has often pointed out, the underlying goal for an athlete (as well as a coach) is to train the individual correctly in order to maximize the potential of the central nervous system to produce the desired training effect. As such, the ability of the body's nervous system to appropriately activate the muscles—in the right order, at the right rate, at the right time—is a factor that can be developed through proper training.

CHAPTER 15 ━━━━━━━━━━━━━━━
The Goal System

Every person in the universe has a fitness level. For endurance runners, fitness is measured in terms of their aerobic, anaerobic, and muscular strength. While $v\dot{V}O_2max$, $\dot{V}O_2max$ LTRV running economy, and muscle strength can be measured in a physiology lab, this type of testing is not practical for the majority of those individuals who are training to race in endurance events.

There is, however, one practical test that can evaluate a person's strength in all of the aforementioned physiological variables. This test involves an all-out effort by a runner to travel as many meters that they can in six minutes. All factors considered, this test is relatively simple to administer. All that is needed to do is pick a day when the runner feels good, and the weather is compatible for racing. After a comprehensive warm-up, the runner runs as far as they can on a 400m track in six minutes. Then, the number of meters averaged per minute/second is calculated.

For example, if the runner travels 1900m in six minutes, that translates to running 317m per minute or 5.3m/per second. Such a velocity of running is an athlete's goal-training pace for 3000m.

As a rule, the standard distance for determining the pace for interval training is 400m. In this instance, the athlete would run each 400m @ a velocity of 76 seconds in training for a 9:28 3k. The standard racing distances are 800, 1500m, 1 mile, 3k, 3200m, 5k, and 10k. Several years ago, a number of outstanding endurance runners, such as Roger Bannister, were produced by English club coaches. These coaches used a four-second differential for determining goal-training paces for five of the different distances. In the aforementioned example, this training routine would translate to 80 sec. per 400 for the 5k; 84 sec. for the 10k, and subsequently 72 sec. for the 1500 and 68 sec. for the 800.

Running intervals of 30 sec. to 3.5 min., with a 1:1 rest at these paces, will significantly improve an athlete's fitness level at each given pace. The English Club coaches trained with multi-tiered paces, using five different velocities of running. Initially, they took the core distance, and then used two velocities slower and two velocities faster, with an emphasis on the core distance. For example, for determining the pace for the 800, they used both the pace for the 400, as well as the athlete's level of pure speed plus 1500 and 3k for endurance. On the other end of the training schedule, they used half marathon and marathon for the 10k plus 5k and 3k for faster intervals.

Personally, I have used this method of goal-pace training at all levels of participation with considerable success. For example, when I took over the distance program at U.C.

Davis in 2000, the average 5k time for the top seven men's cross-country runners was 15:08. Employing the goal-pace training system and by adding neuromuscular strengthening exercises, the average time of our runners was by 20 seconds to 14:48. The period of training was January through May.

The women's cross-country team achieved similar results. In fact, a team that utilizes this training system, supplemented with neuromuscular activities, should achieve a 2-percent improvement over a period of five months. In fact, I used this goal system at Humboldt State from 1966-1988 and achieved the following results: 11 National Champions, 64 All American's, one National Cross Country Championship, and three NCAA Cross Country Runners Up.

Goal-Pace Training

As has been noted previously, an athlete's basic speed best determines their potential to race at any distance. For a 100m runner, acceleration occurs over the first 40 meters; their true speed for the next 40m (3.g., 40m to 50m) is indicative of their endurance speed; while their speed for 80-100 meters determines their race time. An athlete's 100m time is indicative of that individual's 400 meter potential, while their 400m time sets the parameters for their 800 meter to 1000 meter race potential.

A human can only race as a specific percentage of that person's basic speed. Basic speed for an endurance runner is their 400 meter speed. An individual's 400 meter time can be determined by their race time at that distance or by performing two 200m time trials with five minutes of test between the two. The sum of the two time trials +3 seconds is a reliable estimate of the runner's ability, for example: 27+29+3 = 59.

Providing that training focuses on forming a base for running skills, speed, development, and fatigue-resistant muscles, a test for 400m speed can be conducted at the end of week four. Science has provided us with a 400m speed production coefficient for 800m to 10k races. Providing that the training scheme concentrates on developing speed endurance during the fifth, sixth, seventh, and eighth week, a reliable test for anaerobic and anabolic fitness is the six- minute run for distance test, which can be administered at the end of the eighth week.

Six-Minute Run Test

The test should be administered on a 400m track on a day when physical conditions are right for racing. The distance completed is relevant to a person's $\dot{V}O_2max$ running velocity, which is the lowest velocity at which $\dot{V}O_2max$ can be produced. The performance corresponds to an athlete's 3k goal-pace training velocity. The six-minute test reveals the magnitude of an athlete's current aerobic capacity, along with the efficiency at which they move at a very high speed.

Another method for determining an athlete's goal pace is to use race results. Race performance is specific to the athlete's fitness level. A proven way for an individual to determine their goal pace is to improve race goal pace by 2 percent. For example, an athlete who averaged 70 seconds per 400 meters, when running the mile, would average 5.7 meters per second. As such, $5.7 \times .02 = 1.14$ $70-1.14 = 68.9$. 68 per 400 would be the athlete's goal pace.

❏ *Conducting the Six-Minute Run Test*

To the extent feasible, the test should be administered on or about the 28th day of practice and then periodically again throughout the season. The running velocity at which a runner performs this test reveals both the magnitude of their current aerobic capacity, along with the efficiency with which they move at very high speeds. For example, if the athlete runs 1900m in six minutes, they are traveling at a 316m per minute running velocity or 5.3m per second. This running velocity is the lowest running velocity at which $\dot{V}O_2max$ occurs and is represented by the symbol $v\dot{V}O_2max$.

Their training routine could entail running intervals of 30 sec to 3.5 min, with 1:1 recovery - 30 sec. For example, 159m - 45 sec = 238m - 60 sec = 318 - 90 sec = 477 - 120 sec = 636 - 180 sec = 954. Subsequently, they should work up to 3000m of intervals (total) per session. Standard track distances may be used. For example: 200 + 5.3 = 32 - 300 = 56 - 400 = 75 - 800 = 2:30. The average for the six-minute run test is the goal pace for the 3k race. Other targeted paces include:

- 1000 = 3:08 minutes
- 1600 pace is the average 400 time - 5 sec = 70 seconds
- 800 pace is 70-5 = 65 seconds
- 400 pace is 65-5 = 60 seconds
- 5k pace is 75 + 5 = 80 seconds
- 10k pace is 80 + 5 = 85 seconds

❏ *Conducting the 400m Run Test*

Arguably, the 400m run test is an even better way to assess an athlete's level of total fitness, as well as a reliable measure for determining their goal-training pace for events of 800m and beyond. This test should be administered on the 15th day of practice. The velocity achieved by an athlete who has performed this test reveals the current basic speed of the endurance runner. Goal training paces for events of 800-10k can be determined by the athlete's 400m time prediction coefficient: 800 = .91-.92, 1500 = .84-.85, 3k = .77-.78, 5k = .75-.76, 10k steeple = .74-.75; for example, 60 sec = 6.7 m/ps goal paces: 800 = 2:13, 1500 = 4:27, 3k = 9:48, 5k = 16:50.

CHAPTER 16

Muscles Matter

For a runner, the supporting role of their muscles, while their foot is on the ground, is the result of isometric or near isometric muscle actions involving the muscular actions that can take place without any shortening of the muscle. The stability of the upper body while running in an efficient manner is the result of the isometric action of the abdominal and lower back muscles. The calf muscle, in its role of absorbing the force of landing, helps accelerate the foot downward to the ground, as the ankle extends, using very little energy through contraction.

When someone considers how many muscles are vital to successful running, it would seem almost axiomatic to recognize the importance of training the neurological aspect of the driver of all this muscular activity. Individuals with excellent muscle contractibility are able to produce higher rates of oxygen consumption and correspondingly higher workloads than those athletes with lesser muscle contractility. This factor can be especially important in intense workouts. The runner who can work at a higher relative percentage of $\dot{V}O_2$max pace and $v\dot{V}O_2$max should be able to produce greater adaptations in the key variables of endurance physiology than those individuals who work at lower percentages.

In other words, higher muscle contractibility potential is an aerobic attribute that determines the power output of the muscles and is an important ingredient in determining aerobic adaptations. Runners whose muscles are capable of fast force production, with rapid, well-coordinated explosive contractions, have a decided advantage in endurance events. Exercise physiologists have shown that 5k velocity is inversely proportionate to foot-strike time. The best 5k runners will be those athletes with the most powerful neuromuscular characteristics that can produce explosive foot strikes.

Six Important Applicable Facts for Distance Runners

- A reduction in foot strike time of 1/300 of a second will reduce 5k time by up to 10 seconds, assuming that stride length is not reduced.
- A reduction of foot-strike time by 1/100 seconds can lower 5k times up to 30 seconds.
- Improving foot-strike time is the answer to faster 5k times once $\dot{V}O_2$max pace and LT have reached a high level.
- Stride rate and length are also important variables in determining 5k potential. The higher the stride rate, the quicker 5k, assuming that stride length was not reduced.

- The faster 5k runners will also have the fastest 20 meter, 50 meter, and 300 meter times.
- Speed is the key ingredient in determining the potential to race at any distance.

Eccentric Muscle Strength

The power for running is generated through eccentric muscular contractions. Furthermore, increasing the level of eccentric strength in key muscles in the leg is one of the best ways to prevent injuries. In fact, eccentric activities in which muscles are forced to lengthen while they simultaneously attempt to shorten, are the cause of many injuries while running.

The hamstring muscles are prime examples. These muscles are involved in attempting to control the forward swing of the leg. When the foreleg reaches its most forward and upward position, the hamstrings become active in pulling back on the leg. The leg, however, continues to move forward, producing considerable eccentric strain.

Downhill running is one of the best activities to strengthen eccentric muscle action, because it puts the quadriceps and abductor muscles under enormous eccentric strain. The quads attempt to control the flexion of the knee under the high impact loads that occur during downhill running, as the body falls farther with each step. Concurrently, the abductors try to restrain the direction of the femur, under intense acceleration force. The actions that involve high eccentric loads may cause delayed muscle soreness (DOMS), as well as have a protective effect from further muscle soreness and injury.

Numerous studies show that three-minute intervals of downhill running are very beneficial. The hamstring muscles are susceptible to injury during the act of running. One running-specific exercise to protect the hamstring from eccentric strain injury is the pistol squat. This exercise is done by sitting on a bench, then standing on one leg and performing repeated one-leg squats. Another exercise in this regard is the Nordic hamstring fall and rebound. Performing three sets of 12, 10, and 8 repetitions, three times per week, has proven to be successful. Bicycle leg swings are also a very effective eccentric muscle strengthening activity.

Other key muscle groups are also exposed to eccentric muscle strain during running. For example, the calf muscle is activated, as dorsiflexion occurs during the stance phase. Furthermore, the muscles in the bottom of the feet are activated eccentrically, as the arch stretches on impact. The most effective way to strengthen the eccentric muscles involved in running, as well as to prevent injuries is to perform running-specific strengthening exercises.

Neuromuscular strengthening is also a key consideration. As such, an athlete's training should include optimizing the coordination of contractions and relaxation of muscles. Ideally, the least amount of force production should be needed to stabilize unnecessary movements, thus allowing all of the muscle energy to be channeled into propulsion. This step involves a systematic process of proprioceptive training, which involves conditioning the neuromuscular system to coordinate all sensory activity to better overall strength, coordination, and muscular balance during athletic performance. A proprioceptor is any of the sensory end organs in the muscles, tendons, etc. that is sensitive to the stimuli originating by the movement of the body or its parts.

The body uses energy to support itself in an upright position, while keeping the ankles and lower legs from collapsing. Balancing the head on top of the shoulders and having the upper body strength to keep the head from moving forward and back and side-to-side saves energy. Dynamic equilibrium helps interconvert kinetic and potential energy. All factors considered, coaches and athletes do not have to understand all of the intricacies of the central nervous system in order to implement neuromuscular training. As such, considerable research has been conducted that confirms that specific exercises can enhance speed, functional muscle strengthening, running economy, and resistance to fatigue.

In reality, all a coach or an athlete needs to do is to incorporate these exercises into a circuit as part of the warm-up and cool-down phases of the workout. Instead of the traditional jogging and static stretching, dynamic movements can be incorporated into the warm-up and cool-down phases of the workout that promote flexibility, strength, and running rhythm. Many of these dynamic activities mimic the act of running and are ballistic in nature, while some are also designed to strengthen the upper body.

A strong upper body and core muscles help an athlete maintain a tall upright posture, as well as eliminate unnecessary movements, during the act of running, thereby enhancing running economy. As such, running skill drills that promote dynamic equilibrium and coordination between turnovers and stride length, with an emphasis on quick on- and off-foot strikes, can greatly improve speed and running efficiency.

Functional Muscle Strengthening

Since muscles do all of the work of running, it would be beneficial to make them as strong as possible in the athlete, while adding very little bulk. Running is accomplished mostly through eccentric muscular contraction. Eccentric muscle contraction entails a situation in which a muscle is exerting a force, while attempting to shorten, and yet ends up elongated by other forces that are acting on the muscle.

Eccentric muscular action, such a running downhill, strains muscles. On the other hand, there is also something about eccentric muscular training that ultimately provides a considerable amount of protection for muscles and tendons. Eccentric muscle contractions recruit more fast-twitch fibers than do concentric contractions.

This set of circumstances occurs because fast-twitch fibers shorten more quickly than slow twitch fibers, which causes an upswing in the stiffness of muscle cells and allows them to store and utilize impact energy more effectively. Exercises, such as a plyometric activity, will also lead to an increase in muscle stiffness. When stiffness increases, the energy cost of running actually decreases. Research strongly indicates that uneconomical runners possess a more compliant running style during ground contact, when compared with energy-efficient runners.

The key muscles and tendons involved in running—Achilles, calf muscle, patellar, quadriceps, gluts, and hamstrings—all are stretched considerably with each foot strike. If these muscles and tendons are lacking in appropriate stiffness, the leg collapses to a degree on impact. If the tissues are stiffened up, the leg is better able to produce optimal amounts of reactive force. As such, functional activities that strengthen the muscles, tendons, and ligaments that do the work of running are an essential part of training.

Functional Muscle Strength Through Neuromuscular Training

All movements in sports are controlled by the central nervous system. As noted previously, any movement begins with a concept in the brain. The brain then sends signals to activate the muscle fibers that are involved in the movement to be performed. The central nervous system controls the intensity and duration of the contraction and the relaxation of the muscle fibers. As such, competing in endurance racing requires fast and efficient running movements.

All factors considered, the American way of life does not prepare youth for the rigors of sports activities. Far too much and far too often, Americans are members of a riding and sitting society, as opposed to a walking and running society. Young girls, especially, tend to have relatively weak muscles in their knees, lower legs, and feet.

Almost all young endurance athletes begin their careers by competing in youth or high school cross-country and track programs. In many of those instances, the muscles that do the work of running are simply not strong enough to absorb the impact of gravity that occurs with each contact with a running surface. More often than not, as has been noted previously, the muscles are not strengthened concurrently with the increase in intensity and volume of work.

Fortunately, coaches have a way that they can coordinate improving an athlete's workload capacity by improving their level of muscle strength—functional muscle strengthening. Functional muscle strengthening involves performing resistance activities that are specific to the act of running. Most functional strengthening activities are done on one leg at a time. Some, however, involve upper-body strengthening, given that a strong upper body can help eliminate unnecessary energy-wasting movements of a runner. Functional muscle training not only strengthens the muscle fibers it also teaches the neuromuscular system to coordinate the contractions of muscle fibers with those fibers that are not contracting, thereby preventing muscle tears and promoting greater agility.

If all of the coaches who work with youth and high school programs could be convinced to incorporate a functional muscle strengthening program, featuring neuromuscular training activities, concurrently with the increase in the intensity and volume of training that they typically integrate into a specific training season, the incidence of injuries among runners cold be greatly decreased. Injuries or the lack of injuries can have a significant impact on the progress of athletes in their efforts to reach their goals. When muscles are weak or fatigued, more and more stress is put on the other support systems of the body, making the athlete more susceptible to fatigue fractures, ruptured ACLs, and other maladies of the lower legs.

CHAPTER 17 ━━━━━━━━━━━━━
Strength Training for a Purpose

The stretch-shortening cycle movement and propulsion during running is produced by what is commonly termed the stretch-shortening cycle, in which a muscle is initially stretched (preactivated) and then recoils. This action produces a snap-back propulsive force that moves the body forward. All factors considered, this cycle has extremely important consequences for running. As such, strength training must be dynamic in order to straighten the muscles to give them more stretch power, as well as more recoil.

Two very effective and practical ways to incorporate strength training into an endurance runner's training scheme is to include these activities in the dynamic warm-ups and cool-downs that are performed by the runner. Another viable method of integrating strength training into a runner's training regimen is through circuit training (i.e., a series of exercises, drills, and running segments), with minimal or no recovery between activities. In that regard, a coach or athlete can create sprint circuits, $\dot{V}O_2max$ circuits, and lactate-conversion circuits, as well as half-marathon and marathon circuits.

Combining strength activities with segments of running allows the athlete to use their body weight as the level of resistance to enhance the strength of their muscle fibers. Strength training, alone, requires lifting 40 to 50 percent of a person's one-rep maximum in order to produce significant improvement in strength. In turn, circuit training keeps the heart rate accelerated sufficiently to supply enough oxygen to the muscle cells that will allow them to adopt and improve the runner's strength. From a training standpoint, pull-up bars and bar-dip bars are absolutely essential tools that should be available in every outdoor practice area. One of the keys to maximize the efforts expended in a circuit workout is for the runner to work all if the muscle groups of their body.

Published research on the neural aspects of endurance running shows that in order to maximize $\dot{V}O_2max$ and performance, endurance runners must train their nervous system in ways that optimize motor unit recruitment. As noted previously, this objective cannot be accomplished simply by engaging in high-volume, sub-maximal running velocities, since motor recruitment is minimal during slow-to-moderate running. On the flip side, running at velocities of 10k race pace and faster recruit more units, periodizing volume and intensity. All factors considered, when training to reach their maximum potential, runners should run as many miles as possible, as fast as possible, without sustaining a training-stopping injury.

$\dot{V}O_2$max improves, and muscle fibers become stronger, when runners are exposed to increases in training intensities and volume for about 21 days. At that point, they need about seven days of relative recovery before continuing. The first three weeks of training should emphasize running hills, improving speed, and developing fatigue-resistant muscle strength. During their fourth week of training, working on the running skills that produce efficient running should be emphasized. Among the training methods that can be employed to achieve such an outcome are running progressions, step-counting, and doing intervals at $\dot{V}O_2$max (e.g., six-minute routine).

CHAPTER 18 ━━━━━━━━━━━━
Lactate Tolerance: Understanding the Basics

Understanding how to teach the body to shuttle lactates back into the muscles for transformation back to energy is important. Understanding the role of lactic acid in running is to know initially that lactate begins with a chemical process called glucoses. Glucoses is a series of 10 different chemical reactions that break down glucose, a simple six-carbon sugar, into a substance called pyruvic acid. The glycolytic conversion of glucose to pyruvic acid quickly provides the energy that a runner's muscles need for exercise.

For the endurance athlete, the most important aspect of glucoses is what happens after the glycolic reactions take place. The pyruvic acid created during glucoses can be guided into a complex series of energy-creating reaction referred to as the Krebs cycle. This process also metabolizes fats into energy. The Krebs cycle accounts for 90 percent of the energy needed for training to compete in longer endurance races. While the muscles contain instant energy, in the form of A.T.P., it will deplete within 10 to 15 seconds when a runner is exercising vigorously.

After a period of time, the oxygen must mix with A.T.P in order to provide continuous energy. When a runner exercises vigorously for more than 10 to 15 seconds, pyruvic acid is produced, via glycolytic conversion at relatively high rates. When pyruvic acid accumulates faster than the Krebs cycle is able to recycle, a considerable amount of pyruvic acid has to wait in the bloodstream, until it can be processed into energy by additional glucoses.

Lactate should not be blamed for either the burning sensation that sometimes occurs in the working muscles or the soreness, which occasionally follows after a prolonged exercise period. Once the exercise is complete, lactic acid depletes in a few minutes. Developing the ability to convert this lactate will help the athlete run faster for a longer period of time. Developing the process by which lactate is filtered into the muscle cells is commonly referred to as the lactate shuttle.

The lactate shuttle illustrates the fact that lactate is not just a byproduct of glucoses, but is also a high-octane fuel that helps the muscle cells meet their immediate energy requirements. In addition, the body also uses lactate to store excess energy for further use. The velocity of running that causes lactate to build up faster than it can be processed back to pyruvic acid is called the lactate threshold running velocity (LTRV). The velocity with which this occurs is a measure of the amount of oxygen the athlete processes to their muscle cells and the level of efficiency in their mitochondria to convert pyruvic to energy. Mitochondria are minute motor units within each muscle cell in which aerobic energy is produced, with the help of aerobic exercise. If an athlete's LTRV is reached at a relatively low level of speed, it simply means that the oxidative energy system in their muscles is not very efficient.

A key goal of an athlete's training regimen should be to progressively raise their LTRV to higher speeds. Beginning runners need to systematically build on their glycogenic system and lactate shuttle system concurrently. Emphasizing work that promotes lactate shuttle efficiency will greatly enhance the advancement of the glucoses process. When an athlete runs, the feeling of discomfort is a result of them running faster than their current LTRV, more so than that of a poor level of $\dot{V}O_2max$.

As such, improving their lactate shuttle system should receive a high priority in an athlete's scheme of training for participating in endurance racing events. From day one, a key goal of their training to race in endurance events should be to progressively move their LTRV to higher and higher speeds. Doing so will mean that their operative energy system is improving and that their muscles are getting better at pulling lactate out of the blood and converting it to energy.

The ability of the muscles to take lactate from the blood depends on a protein conversion process (monocarbonate transporter). The protein involved in this process, which is found on the outer edges of muscle membrane, can help transport lactate from the blood into the interior of the muscle cells. The more MCTI concentrations, the faster that lactate can be converted into energy and the higher should an athlete's LTRV be.

Research indicates that fairly intense training is better than volumes of moderate intensities to improve LTRV. In fact, an athlete who runs at velocities higher than their present level of LTRV can improve their LTRV as much as 20 percent over the course of four to six months. Intense training also improves the concentration of a key mitochondrial enzyme in the body called cytochrome. Found within the mitochondrial, cytochrome is critically important oxidative enzymes that are linked to cap swings on LTRV. High intensity workouts involving fairly heavy doses of sprint work have been shown to advance an athlete's level of LTRV. Arguably, an exceptional lactate threshold workout would involve doing the following: three minutes at $v\dot{V}O_2max$; three-minute rest; 1,000 at $v\dot{V}O_2max$; rest, and then sprint work at 800-600- 400-200 meter paces.

CHAPTER 19 ━━━━━━━━━━━━━━

Neuromuscular Power, Speed, and Efficiency: Understanding the Basics

Neuromuscular characteristics are key components in racing any distance. Quick feet are as important in the 5k as they are in the 100m. An endurance runner whose muscles are capable of fast force production with rapid, well-coordinated, explosive contractions, has a definite edge in racing, given that racing velocity is inversely proportionate to foot-strike time. The less time the foot is in contact with the surface, the faster the athlete is able to race.

Foot-strike time is a function of how quickly the runner's muscles react to surface impact, how rapidly the gastric and anterior tibias stabilize the ankle that is controlling dorsiflexion and plantar flexion, and how fast the foot can leave the surface during the stance phase. Even though quick feet are extremely important in racing, they are often almost totally ignored as a coaching tool. As such, an athlete should create as much neuromuscular power as possible.

The two major aspects for creating neuromuscular power are running skills and running-specific muscle strengthening. As noted previously, with proper coaching in these areas, an endurance runner can improve their basic performance speed. Basic performance speed is the single most important physiological variable in determining how fast someone can race at any distance. With correct frontside and backside running mechanics, an athlete can position their feet to strike the running surface as far back under the center of mass as possible, which results in a quick on- and off-the-surface foot strike, while keeping turnover at 98 per minute.

Running-specific strengthening of the muscles that perform the work of running will cause them to become more fatigue-resistant, as well as greatly improve their level of speed endurance. Creating neuromuscular power is equally as important in racing in events of 800-10k, as is creating cardiovascular power. Possessing a high $\dot{V}O_2max$ and lactate threshold running velocity will not produce the complete runner. These physiological assets must be complimented by an appropriate level of neuromuscular development, if a runner is going to hold a race pace, cover surges, and be able to answer the finishing kicks of other runners.

When I coached at UC Davis, we used the pool for cross training, and I had numerous conversations with the swim coach. We discussed the similarity of training between his stroke- counting method, and my turnover-counting technique. He had a watch that could be set to determine the number of a swimmer's strokes per second or minute. I purchased one and started clocking my runners' turnovers.

Subsequently, I carried the watch with me to meets to check on elite runners. Later on, I did some work with Lindsey Haight, four-time CIF State champion in the 800m, as well as with other topflight athletes. Her turnover was 98 per minute when doing interval work, which would increase to 102 during her kick.

Michael Johnson's turnover at 300m was 118, almost two per second, when running a sub-45s 400. His stride length computed to be close to 8', when he ran with a full range of motion. Gabe Jennings also had a turnover of 118, but his stride was only 7', due to the fact that he did not run with a full range-of- motion stride cycle. Bob Kennedy, Adam Goutcher, and Steve Scott all had turnovers of 96, when running at race-goal paces. Michael Stember's turnover in high school was at only 90, but later he picked it up to 96 at Stanford. An elite Kenyan, when setting a world's best in the marathon, was counted at 98 per minute, numerous times throughout the run.

Running with a full range of motion shows a stride cycle in which the heel is brought up under the buttock, until the calf muscle collapses against the hamstring, forming the shortest angle possible between the lower and upper leg. This factor accounts for a quick return of the foot to the ground. Elite Kenyans and Ethiopians have similar stride cycle and turnover rates. During the final sprint, they speed up by increasing their turnover rate. In contrast, most American elite runners seem to try to run faster by increasing their stride length. Subsequently, they tend to fade, because it is less economical.

As noted previously, all aspects of running are controlled by the brain. The brain can be prepared to reproduce running skills that produce a powerful and efficient foot strike and a turnover of 97-98 per minute. A powerful foot strike begins with the foot striking the running surface on the flexible part of the foot, as far under a runner's center of mass as possible.

When the upper leg reaches its most forward and upper position, the hamstring halts the motion and brings the lower leg and foot down to the surface under the torso. This action is actually made possible, when the foot pushes off the ground and brought directly under the buttock by collapsing the calf muscle against the hamstring. As the foot strikes the surface, all of the kinetic chain from the glutes down through the big toes engage in the stretch cycle. The runner's center of mass is directly over the flexible part of the foot.

Energy is stored, in the amount of 2.5 times the runner's weight. As the center of mass moves ahead of the foot, the stretch-shortening action of the kinetic chain snaps back, providing the force for forward movement. Very little energy is wasted during this movement. Although some energy is used to maintain balance, the stretch-reflex action is very economical, when the foot is moving downward at contact. If the foot is moving forward when it hits the surface, it will cause a heel-first contact, as well as a braking action, before the snapback can occur. The further down under the center of mass occurs, the quicker and more dynamic the stretch-shortening phenomenon happens, and the greater the power created with each touchdown.

The stride cycle is broken down into two phases—frontside mechanics and backside mechanics. The foot is the lever that applies the force. The contour of the foot is such that it plays an important role in applying force. The foot should make first contact with the surface, immediately in front of the heel bone and slightly to the outside foot, producing a slight pronation. Then, as the body weight moves forward, a slight supination takes place. This action literally screws the foot into the surface, complementing the snapback action of the kinetic chain.

Backside mechanics begin as the big toes push off releasing the energy. The farther the foot is allowed to continue its backward motion, the longer the lever that has to be brought forward during the stride cycle. Elite runners minimize this backward follow-through and immediately bring the foot up and under the knee, until the calf collapses against the hamstring. A side view of the foot would resemble a wheel pattern, as the heel steps over the knee in its forward movement. Non-elite runners show an ankle-over-mid-shin gait cycle, with a longer lever and a slower return of the foot, which causes the heel to strike first.

The brain can be trained to produce running actions that result in a powerful and economical running gait. This result is achieved by repetitively performing a series of skills and running-specific strength activities. All factors considered, this series is best implemented during the warm-up, while preparing all of the muscles for intense running.

The rhythm of running begins with the athlete's posture and arm action. This factor requires a tall, relaxed body, with the head and shoulders directly over the hips. The arms hang loosely from the shoulders, with the upper and lower arms forming a 90-degree angle. The shoulder and face muscles must be completely relaxed, as this allows drive forward and backward. The hands are closed lightly, with the thumbnails pointing upward.

As the arms move forward, the angle is shortened slightly, with the hands stopping at midline at the top and at the hip on the bottom. The emphasis is in driving the elbows, with the muscles in the lower arm totally relaxed. Repetitions of arm movements in which the tempo is gradually accelerated until relaxation is no longer possible will promote complete relaxation of the arms and shoulder muscles.

The rhythm of running shows the arms and feet moving in synchronized harmony. The quicker the arm movement, the quicker the foot strike and turnover. The longer the arm swing, the longer the stride. When the arch of the foot is completely stretched, and the center of mass is directly over it, the heel is lifted allowing the stretch shortening cycle to release the stored energy as the big toes push downward.

This power-producing action can be reinforced with drills performed in a speed agility ladder. A speed agility ladder is 20' in length with 14" spacing. Quick feet and correct foot actions can be taught with this instrument. To use this tool, the athlete should assume a correct running posture and then begin walking through the ladder. When moving over the ladder, the athlete places their entire foot on the ground, then lifts their heel, pushing off with their toes, while stepping one ankle over the other. The 14" spacing is designed to teach the foot strike to occur directly under the center of mass. Subsequently, this action should be repeated while increasing the tempo to its upmost.

A relaxed upper body and quick relaxed arm action should accompany the footwork. Good posture and quick relaxed arm action coordinates with the foot action. The brain can further enhance an athlete's running skills by performing repetitions on the hash marks on a football field or placing flat sticks 3' apart.

After learning to run with a restricted stride length, the next step is for an athlete to advance to using an acceleration ladder. An acceleration ladder consists of eight flat sticks, amid several 3" hurdles, with a spacing of 1.5', 2', 2.5', 3', 3.5', 4', 4.5', and 5'. The 3" hurdles are used to complete the 5' pattern through 30m. This ladder allows the athlete to increase their stride length, while keeping the foot strike under their center of mass.

Teaching the brain to produce powerful, economical running must be accompanied with building strong fatigue-resistant working muscles. All factors considered, the better the running technique and the stronger the muscles, the better the runner's performance. Developing strong fatigue-resistant muscles is best accomplished through running-specific strength activities. Running-specific strength activities mimic some phase of the running gait.

After initially completing the 30 meters of the acceleration ladder, the athlete should continue running using a 5' stride length and quick feet. When an athlete becomes proficient with a 5' stride, they should continue the pattern to a total run of 50 meters. Performing repetitions of this ladder has been shown to improve basic speed and running efficiency. By extending the run beyond 50m, an athlete can learn to hold a fast-relaxed pace for a longer period of time (e.g., 50m, 100m, 150m, and 250m). Doing the ladder skill drills three days per week will help program the brain to produce powerful and efficient running. An alternative to performing the ladder drills is a session focused on running progressions.

CHAPTER 20 ━━━━━━━━━━━━━━
Running Progressions

In order to help teach the muscles of their athletes to adhere to the appropriate pattern of recruitment and firing, coaches utilize a variety of techniques. One of the most effective, in that regard, is the use of running progressions, which entail the following directives:

- Assume a tall relaxed posture and then begin the relaxed arm movement, as previously described. Gradually increase the arm tempo with complete relaxation.
- Move the arms at a moderate tempo and then lift the heel and rise on the toes, activating the flexible part of the foot. Gradually increase the tempo until the runner can no longer remain relaxed.
- Stand tall and begin arm movement and then begin lifting the heels, rocking up on to the toes, while increasing the tempo to the limit. Begin arm movement and then start running in place, using the flexible part of the foot. Increase the tempo, while lifting the heels higher and higher under the buttock. Continue until the calf collapses against the hamstring and complete relaxation can no longer be maintained. Repeat several times.
- Walk with quick feet, using an ankle-over-ankle quickstep action for 10m and then continue with the running action for 10m. Advance to ankle-over-mid-shin for 10m. Finally, advance to ankle-over-knee running action for 20 seconds.

The coach can alternate this running progression with the ladders. Both activities can be incorporated into a dynamic warm-up. A dynamic warm-up activates all of the muscle groups of an athlete and prepares them for intense running. Dynamic warm-ups can be created by either the coach or the athlete by combining running skills with full-body muscle strengthening activities that strengthen the upper body and the core, as well as the muscles that do the work of running.

Most strengthening exercises can be executed, using the athlete's own bodyweight as the resistance. Because track & field and cross country are outdoor activities, it makes for better continuity in a practice session, when the strength activities that are part of the training regimen can be conducted at the same venue. When the weather forces practice indoors, many activities combining running skills and running specific strength activities can be created.

Planning workouts to develop the complete endurance athlete can be a complicated task. The distances of 800m, 10m, 3k, 5k, 10k, and marathon are recognized as the basic competitive distances for endurance racers. Competitors in any of these distances must incorporate all of the physiological fundamentals of training in order to become a complete competitor. Running speed, efficiency, and fatigue-resistant muscle strength must be developed, concurrently with $\dot{V}O_2max$ and the lactate shuttle system. Not only must coaches and athletes decide what workouts to do, they must also determine in what sequence such workouts should be inserted in the periodization of training.

It should be kept in mind that training to race at any distance is a matter of stressing muscle fibers and then allowing them to rest and adapt to a particular level of stress. If an athlete's training is periodized, based on improving speed and strength, all of the cardiovascular and neuromuscular variables of training can be systematically developed.

It is important to note that coaches in the United States and most of the Western Hemisphere appear to be totally dedicated to developing $\dot{V}O_2max$, with a mileage quota of easy-to-moderate running velocities, before adding any of the other training fundamentals to their scheme. Age-group, high school, collegiate, and even coaches of elite runners began their training seasons by developing an aerobic base first, before addressing the other fundamentals.

Italian Coach Renata Conava, who developed Olympic Marathon champions Gelando Borden and Stefano Baldine, as well as coaching many Kenyan elite runners, does not adhere to this line of thinking. He does not start his training season by building an aerobic base, but rather by building strength and explosive muscular actions. Hill work and short, fast intervals prevail in the first few weeks of training. Young Kenyan hopefuls train at lactate threshold running velocities early in their development.

As noted previously, science has shown that a person's basic speed is the best determiner of that individual's racing potential. Furthermore, an athlete's $\dot{V}O_2max$ has a low rating in that regard. Why not begin a training season by first developing speed and muscular strength? Workouts that enhanced these two variables also jump start $\dot{V}O_2max$, LTRV, and running economy.

If an athlete's training season is periodized by improving the individual's skills, strength, and speed, the season can be broken down into four categories:

❑ *Category 1:*

In this phase, the athlete is taught to run with power and efficiency. This stage begins with developing proper frontside and backside mechanics. As this is being done, the athlete learns to run fast-relaxed for short segments. Subsequently, the length of each segment that can be completed fast-relaxed is then extended. If hills are available, running short, steep inclines at an all-out fast-relaxed effort will add power to the working muscles. Running gradually inclining hills at a 5k effort in three-minute segments with 1:1 rest, adds strength to the working muscles, as well as improving the athlete's $\dot{V}O_2max$ and the lactate shuttle system. Hill running can also make an athlete psychologically tougher, when they continue to push the pain barrier higher and higher.

❏ *Category 2:*

Running-specific strengthening workouts, consisting of resistance exercises that mimic the biomechanics of running, will add more force to the ground with each step, thereby conditioning the muscles to become more fatigue-resistant. The working muscles must be strengthened throughout the entire training and racing season, so that the highest percentage of quality work possible can be done.

❏ *Category 3:*

The more an athlete trains at race-goal pace, the more efficient their neuromuscular system becomes at continuing that pace for longer periods of time. In order to continue to improve race times, an athlete must also run at velocities that are faster than race pace, as well as some that are slower than race pace, so that they can improve their basic speed and endurance.

If an athlete is an 800m specialist, they need to run some true speed and 400m velocities to improve their running power. They also need to do some 1500m and 3k training to develop greater strength and speed endurance. This system, called multi-tiered training, was developed by British Club coaches in the 1940s and 1950s. In fact, numerous world records have been set by British Club members using this system.

❏ *Category 4:*

Tapering, i.e., reducing volume and adding real speed, about 10 days prior to the most important races of the season is a must for optimal performance. Rest and running rhythm are of the utmost importance at this time. The last excruciatingly hard workout should be conducted about 10 days prior to the climax of the season and coincide with the end of the 21-day stress cycle. After this, the volume of training should be reduced 30 percent or more, but the intensity of this training maintained. A complete rest of about 48 hours prior to race day, with a few rhythm reps at a 3k pace should do the trick.

The Science of Training to Race in Endurance Events

In recent years, a number of endurance runners have begun to place even more emphasis on training in a "scientific way." In fact, two new books have been published that shed light on the scientific basis for training to compete in endurance races— *Running Science* and *The Science of Running*. Both books debunk many of the myths associated with training for endurance events and provide an overview of scientific facts about the physiology of training for endurance runners.

Every runner, regardless of their age or fitness level, has the same basic needs. As such, they need to improve their basic speed, perfect their running skills, and develop their level of running-specific muscle strength. Running a race of any distance is, first and foremost, a neuromuscular activity, with the cardiovascular system of the body playing a supportive role. Foot-strike time, turnover rate, and stride length are the critical determining factors of racing potential, as opposed to the cardiovascular variables.

The neurovascular system consists of the brain, spinal cord, and nerves that stimulate muscular action. In order to complete volumes of intense running, the muscles must be strengthened sufficiently to withstand the stress imposed on them. Furthermore, the neuromuscular system of the body must receive equal training time, as does the cardiovascular system. As such, strength training can be easily incorporated into the warm-up and cool-down phases of an athlete's daily workout, along with running-specific strength activities. In fact, extra strength sessions can be added to recovery-day workouts.

The brain controls muscle contractions, respiration, and heart rate. Accordingly, a training scheme to train the brain is what the athlete needs. Every step taken, whether it is quick and efficient or slow and energy inefficient, is recorded in the brain. Teaching running skills that produce proper frontside and backside mechanics can be recorded and reproduced by the brain.

A training scheme that is designed to enhance the ability of an athlete to learn a core to run with power and efficiency is desirable. Along with running-specific strength exercises, such a scheme will stimulate the body's cardiovascular and neuromuscular systems to produce optimal race performances. Muscle contractions stimulate the heart to beat faster, thereby speeding up circulation and consequently sending more fuel to the muscle cells.

As noted previously, running is a neuromuscular activity first and cardiovascular action second. Unfortunately, while developing the neuromuscular system is vital to an endurance runner's potential, the factor is virtually ignored by most coaches and athletes. Coaches and athletes are so absorbed with mileage quotas, coming up with the magic interval session and tempo runs, that they fail to teach proper foot strike and provide the athlete with fatigue-resistant muscle strength.

Strengthening the kinetic chain, from the buttocks down through the toes, will produce a quick and powerful foot strike. The quicker the foot gets on and off the ground, the more power created. All endurance athletes, regardless of their experience or ability, have the same basic physiological requirements, when training to race in endurance events.

CHAPTER 21

Principles of Training to Race in Endurance Events

Successfully training to race in endurance events involves a number of factors, including adherence to the following principles:

- Learning to run with power and efficiency should be the focal point of any training scheme, with running skills and fatigue-resistant strength activities incorporated into the workouts.
- Learning to run fast-relaxed and then extending that distance as far as possible is essential to racing at any distance. Foot-strike time, stride rate, and stride length are specific to race time, while vVO_2max is not.
- Basic speed is the physiological variable that most determines an athlete's potential to race at any distance.
- An individual's 400m time is the basic speed for endurance athletes. Improving their 400m time will significantly improve an athlete's potential to race at longer distances.
- Even beginning runners should do short segments of speed work. The first step taken in a workout should be a fast one.
- Being able to hold a specific pace for the longest possible time is the key to racing at goal pace.
- Fatigue-resistance muscle strengthening determines the length of time that an athlete can maintain a specific running velocity. This factor is best accomplished by performing running-specific strength exercises that strengthen the kinetic chain.
- The focal point of any training scheme should be to strengthen the neuromuscular system of the body, given that it is muscular functions that bring the torso to the finish line. Neuromuscular actions stimulate the heart and circulatory system to produce energy for the muscles to do their work. On the other hand, no cardiovascular activity occurs until a muscular contraction occurs.
- The brain controls the intensity and duration of muscular activities. It also coordinates the contraction and relaxation of the muscle fibers and the functioning of the respiratory system. In addition, it facilitates the distribution of "fuel" (energy) to the muscle cells. Training the brain is, arguably, one of the most important components of a regimen for successful racing.
- The neuromuscular system and the cardiovascular system must be strengthened concurrently, with equal training time given to each.

The periodization of a training scheme should be based on scientific evidence. In fact, ample evidence exists to show that both muscle fibers and $\dot{V}O_2$max will gain in strength with about 21 days of exposure to systematically increased volume and intensity. They then need about seven days to adapt to the stress and adaptation phenomena. This schedule makes a training period of approximately 28 days very effective, as well as practical.

An athlete's fitness level will be highest at the end of the 21 days of accelerated effort. To the degree possible, important races should be scheduled when a person's fitness level is at its highest. The typical training and competitive season for entry-level athletes is dictated by the school's calendar and lasts about four months.

During the first 28-day period of training, workouts should concentrate on developing the running skills that produce the powerful foot strike and the efficient use of fuel. During this period, running-specific strength activities that promote fatigue-resistant muscle strength can also be incorporated into an athlete's workouts. Daily running workouts should feature 400m training, as well as developing a base for improving basic speed. Learning to run fast-relaxed should be an important goal for this period of training.

During the second 28-day period of training, efforts should be made to work on extending the distance that an athlete can run fast-relaxed. The development of speed endurance would feature 800m and 1500m training. These paces can be based on 400m time: 800 GP = .92-.93 percent, 1500 GP = .86-.87 percent, 800 + 500m running pace, which helps develop a full range of motion stride cycle and jump-starts the $\dot{V}O_2$max and lactate conversion process.

The six-minute run test should be conducted at the end of the eighth week. The 3k, 5k, and 10k goal pace should then be calculated, based on the test results. The number of meters averaged per second is equivalent to the $\dot{V}O_2$max pace, plus the 3k pace. Then, four seconds per 400m for 5k and eight seconds per 400 for 10k should be added. To determine the goal pace for the 500m and the 800m, four seconds and eight seconds should be subtracted, respectively. After improving their basic speed and level of speed endurance, the training can then concentrate on improving their $\dot{V}O_2$max and LTRV, during weeks 9-12. Not only will LTRV workouts significantly improve an athlete's production of aerobic fuel, it will also develop their level of strength endurance.

Improving strength endurance will increase an athlete's capability to sustain race-goal pace for longer periods of time. Training velocities for $\dot{V}O_2$max 5k and 10k, which are featured during this training period, will ensure greater aerobic power. Athletes should remember that they must continue to improve their basic speed and level of fatigue-resistant muscle strength throughout the entire season.

Weeks #13, 14, 15, and 16

At this time of the season, the coach and athletes should be able to determine the best potential race distance for each athlete. Workouts for the remainder of the season should feature running at race-goal paces. Numerous studies show that the more volume ran at a specific velocity, the more the athlete's potential to race at that particular velocity. While athletes can concentrate to train at specific paces, they also need to train at paces faster than race pace, as well as some that are slower and longer to ensure that their speed and endurance are not neglected.

Variable pace training is also very valuable at this time. Variable pace running is running at different velocities within the same interval. Ten days before the big race of the year, coaches should require their athletes to perform the final quality workout before the race. For example: 3x 400 at a mile pace, 60-second active rest, three minutes easy x3 sets, and then 1x 400 at an all-out pace. The last five days before the big race would entail rhythm reps (e.g., 200m-400m) at $\dot{V}O_2$max and some real speed work. The volume of training by the athlete should be reduced by 30 percent. The athlete should also and get plenty of rest over the last 48 hours before the race. It is essential that athletes have confidence in their level of fitness and race to that level.

Planning Daily and Weekly Workouts

Practice sessions of about 90 minutes fit nicely into the daily routine of most athletes. Ninety minutes allows time for housekeeping duties, as well as ample time for conditioning. A workout involves four basic phases:

❏ *Phase #1: Warm-Up*

This part of the daily routine should prepare all of the muscle groups of an athlete for intense running. A warm-up should not begin with jogging, since this would help ingrain a slow turnover and foot-strike pattern on the brain. Instead, warm-ups should be dynamic and consist of running skills and running-specific strength activities. In reality, a warm-up can last for 30-40 minutes and can be a mini-workout within itself.

❏ *Phase #2: Skill Work*

Teaching proper frontside and backside running mechanics is essential to producing power, as well as efficient, full range-of-motion running. This aspect is an everyday must of training. While it can be incorporated into the warm-up, it can, in fact, occur throughout conditioning work. Running progressions are a vital part of this phase.

❑ *Phase #3: Speed Work*

Performing speed work at intervals of 30 seconds to 3.5 minutes at $\dot{V}O_2max$ pace, 5k, and 10k goal pace will help ensure both a high $\dot{V}O_2max$ and an enhanced level of LTRV. This phase of the workout can last up to 45 minutes and cover up to 5000m of running.

❑ *Phase #4: Cool-Down*

Cool-downs should not be designed to increase the daily mileage of an athlete. Rather, they should entail striding, functional strength activities, and stretching.

The Weekly Plan

A mileage quota should not be set for athletes. Instead, each workout should be planned to accomplish a specific goal, with as much quality work as possible. Rotating daily workouts, based on the activation of different types of muscle fibers, will allow a quality workout every day. Recovery days are best implemented with cross training and running-specific strength activities. Not only does performing easy runs on recovery days fail to improve an athlete's racing potential, they also further ingrain the brain with neuromuscular patterns that accentuate slow turnover and foot strike, thereby making an athlete very efficient at slow running.

If an athlete's training scheme is periodized with running skills, running-specific strength exercises, and a foundation for speed, the athlete can develop both their cardiovascular and neuromuscular systems concurrently and develop them to the fullest. One of the most important objectives of this type of periodization training is the full development of the stretch shortening cycle—a reflex phenomenon.

The Stretch Shortening Cycle—A Reflex Phenomenon

Movement and propulsion during running are produced by what is commonly referred to as the stretch shortening cycle (SSC). As previously noted, in this cycle, a leg muscle is first stretched (pre-activated) and then it recoils, producing with each snapback the propulsive force that moves the body forward. When the body's weight (force of gravity) collapses the foot, all of the kinetic chain goes on stretch (pre-activated), storing energy equal to up to 2.5 times the runner's weight. As the center of mass moves ahead of the foot, the entire kinetic chain snaps back, releasing the stored energy.

The fact that the stretch shortening cycle provides force for forward movement dictates that running-specific strength activities are essential to strength training for running, as well as for pure running training. The actions of the runner's hamstrings during running illustrate how the stretch shortening cycle operates. It is a common belief by coaches and athletes that the hamstrings move the body ahead by contracting, while the foot is on the ground.

In reality, the hamstring muscles are actually only slightly active during the first two-thirds of the stance and are totally inactive during the last one-third of the stance, when they are supposedly providing force for forward movement. The hamstring's role in providing force is being stretched (pre-activated) during the forward swing and then recoiling elastically. This action does not entail eccentric muscular contraction; it is the stretch shortening cycle in operation.

The hamstrings provide the breaking force during the forward swing and prepare the leg for contact with the ground. Hamstring and thigh curls, performed while in a sitting position, do nothing to strengthen them for running. Bicycle leg swings, runner's pose with a stretch cord, and eccentric falls are among the running-specific exercises that help strengthen the hamstrings in a running manner.

The gastrocnemius (calf-muscle) is another contributor to the stretch shortening cycle. Barely active during the last one-third of the stance, the gastrocnemius employs elastic energy to aid forward movement. Heel raises are used to strengthen the gastroc, but not in a running sense. Falls to earth with forward hops is a more running specific strengthening exercise.

The problem that Americans have with the muscles of their legs lies in their roots. To begin with, America is a riding nation, whereas the countries that produce most of the medals in endurance racing are natives of walking and running societies. By walking or running to school, church, work, visit relatives, and play, young people in these countries develop a base for having strong leg muscles. By the time they are of high school age, their working muscles are as strong as American collegiate runners.

Adding to the problematic issue is the fact that when the young American males decide to compete in athletic events, those individuals with the best basic speed and athletic ability tend to be siphoned off into football and soccer. The same factor is true with young females, with soccer and volleyball. More often than not, what the cross-country coach gets is mostly the bottom of the athletic chain.

When track season rolls around, the head coach wants to determine where the talent lies in the new team. The coach then has a time trial in the 100m. The top four or five become sprinters, the next athletes in line (performance-wise) become hurdlers and jumpers. The heaviest members typically become throwers.

The coach in charge of developing the 800, 1600, and 3200 runners gets the rest of the pool of candidates. This coach then further impedes the basic speed of their potential endurance race performers by sending them out to build up minutes of running, with little or no instructions on proper running mechanics, as well as no functional muscle strengthening to prepare their muscles for running.

The *Track & Field Omnibook* offers the following advice concerning distance runners: "I'd start (them) jogging twice a week for five minutes, then 10, 20, 30, minutes, initially three times a week, and then daily. I'd do it on a time-and-fun basis. Distance runners develop primarily by simple progressive increments of enjoyable running." This advice is the basic theory of training that is followed by entry-level coaches throughout the U.S. The theory is for athletes to start easy and slow, and then build toward faster running.

Given their own means of interpreting what constitutes proper running form, entry-level athletes will, with few exceptions, develop a running rhythm that features overstriding, with a slow turnover and foot strike. As the number of minutes of slow running is increased, the athlete becomes neuromuscularly adapt at running slow. The slow-to-fast theory of developing entry-level athletes defies the fact that speed is the most important physiological factor in determining a person's ability to race at any distance.

Somewhere during the latter part of the training season, the coach may finally decide that in order to race, it might be necessary to develop some speed in the athlete. Since it takes several weeks of specific training to improve basic speed, it is too late to be truly effective for that season. Furthermore, in many instances, the coach has not spent enough training time conditioning the muscles that do the work of running to withstand this new stress and injury rates.

The obvious solution to producing better elite runners in this country is for the powers that be in track & field, i.e., the USATF Coaches Education Committee, to come up with a training scheme in which entry-level athletes are taught to run with power and efficiency and to develop strong, fatigue-resistant working muscles. If the young hopefuls in distance running could be exposed to heavy doses of these types of activities for the first 10 years of their running development, they would be a more complete runner (i.e., having both speed and strength) by the time they become emerging elite athletes. As noted previously, a runner must have fatigue-resistant working muscles that can sustain speed-endurance paces for long periods of time, as well as still be able to sprint at the end of a race.

Basic speed is the most important single factor in 400m performance. In fact, a close relationship exists between 100m time and 400m time and 400m time with the 800, 1500, 3k, 5k, and 10k performance.

Lee Evans, in the *Track & Field Omnibook*, tenders the following advice for runners: "Run as fast as possible, while staying completely relaxed. The ultimate competitor is one who learns how to sustain an all-out fast, relaxed effort for the entire distance." In reality, medals in the World and Olympic Games endurance races go to the athletes who can run the fastest when they're fatigued. They are the best in the world, because they have learned to run fast-relaxed during their development from entry level.

Learning to run fast-relaxed is a factor of neuromuscular training. Unfortunately, until the leaders in the profession of coaching endurance runners change their concept of the physiological aspects of developing the complete endurance athlete, the United States will never gain prominence in this area.

Until American coaches and athletes discard the myth that an athlete must establish an aerobic-base with sub-maximal-paced running, before adding other physiological aspects of training, the United States is doomed to lag behind in the world of endurance running. In order to change, Americans must build their training scheme around teaching entry-level athletes how to run with power and efficiency and build strong, fatigue-resistant leg muscles. When this step is accomplished, all of the other physiological systems involved in running can be jump-started, as well as the cardiovascular and neuromuscular aspects of running developed.

The faster an athlete's 400m time, the greater the potential to race in endurance events of 800m-10k. Accordingly, improving an athlete's 400m time should be at the top of the list of factors that should be addressed when planning workouts. In order to continually improve basic speed, the athlete must be taught to run with power and efficiency. This learning process must be combined with developing strong, fatigue-resistant working muscles, mainly the core, buttocks, quads, and hamstrings.

The basic element of improving real speed is to learn to run fast-relaxed. In order to improve speed, an athlete must eliminate as much backside mechanics as possible, while increasing their frontside mechanics, as much as possible. If coaches accept the fact that basic speed determines an athlete's potential to race any distance, why do coaches in the USA wait until later in the season to develop this factor? Why not make the very first step of the training period a fast one?

Young, unconditioned, entry-level athletes are capable of running short, fast distances from the very beginning of their development. Short, fast intervals, accompanied by functional muscle strengthening, will form a base for all of the other physiological aspects of training. In reality, the greater the stress on the muscles, the greater the stress on the heart.

Coaches are aware of the neuromuscular aspects of training, but either do not understand this aspect or choose to ignore it. The neurological aspects of training entail learning to run with power and efficiency and the functionally strengthening the muscles that do the work of running. In fact, running skills must be one of the first things a coach teaches endurance-running hopefuls. Furthermore, this focus on running skills should be continued on a daily basis throughout the entire season—in fact, over an athlete's entire running career.

Gold Medal Running Form

All Gold Medal winners of endurance running events in the World and Olympic Games exhibit similar running characteristics, e.g., a tall, relaxed torso with the head and shoulders directly over the hips. As noted previously, the arms move with a short, quick, forward-and-backward motion. The foot strike should be quick, as the foot is driven back under the center of mass. The side view of the foot cycle resembles that of a wheel. The running action encompasses a full range of motion, with an ankle-over-knee recovery. In reality, entry-level endurance runners can be taught to emulate Gold Medal running form.

Speed-Agility Ladder

One of the surest ways to teach a runner the proper foot placement is by using a speed-agility ladder. Using a speed-agility ladder, which is approximately 20 ft. long, with rungs placed every 4', is fairly straightforward. The first step for an athlete to use this ladder is to imagine that they have a rod sticking through each ankle. They then walk through the ladder by lifting the heel and stepping one ankle over the other, while flexing the toes backwards. This walking action can help teach the muscles to place the foot strike under the center of mass. The walking action should be performed six times, while increasing the walking tempo each time through the ladder. Subsequently, this action can substitute running for walking. Similar to before, the tempo should be increased each time through the ladder.

An athlete should work toward running as fast as possible, while keeping their foot strike within the confines of the ladder rungs. To further program the feet to move faster, the athlete could be required to progress through the ladder by stepping in and out of the ladder as fast as possible (two feet in—two feet out), while advancing through it. Next, the athlete should face north and do the same quick-foot action, while advancing through the ladder laterally, and then returning facing south.

The quickstep run can also be done on the hash marks of a football field or by placing flat sticks a yard apart. When working on a speed-agility ladder, the athlete should practice good posture and perform quick, relaxed arm movements.

Acceleration Ladder

The next step in learning the progression of running is to work with an acceleration ladder. This ladder systematically increases the stride length, while keeping the foot strike under the center of mass. For the first eight steps, the athlete should use flat sticks set apart at distances of 1.5', 2', 2.5', 3', 3.5', 4', 4.5', and 5'. Beginning athletes should work up to 4', and then keep a 4' spacing until they become adept at that stride length. For individuals who can advance beyond a 4' stride, the settings would be increased to 5' and eventually to 6' (5'-3", 5'-6", 5'-9" and 6').

When a young female athlete can run smoothly using a 5' stride, she will become an accomplished runner, as will a young male with a 6' stride. All factors considered, the most effective acceleration ladder is laid out with flat sticks for the first eight strides and then with 3" risers to a distance of 30m, followed by 5" risers to a distance of 45m. The ultimate acceleration ladder advances to 60m, with 7" risers from 45m to 60m.

The running action is a sprint start through the flat sticks, ankle-over mid-shin to 30m and then ankle-over knee for the rest of the ladder. Using a 45m ladder is very practical, because the runner can continue beyond that distance, using muscle memory to complete any distance desired. Athletes should be encouraged to remember to maintain a tall, relaxed posture, with their arms moving fast-relaxed throughout each effort.

Progression of Running, When Ladders Are Not Available

A progression of running can be used to instill muscle memory. In that regard, the athlete should begin by quickstep walking, with an ankle-over-ankle movement, while maintaining good posture and arm action. This action should be performed for 10 seconds x 6. Next, the athlete should walk for 10 seconds and then quickstep run, with ankle-over-ankle foot action, for 10 seconds x 6. Then, the athlete should progress to 10 seconds of ankle-over-mid-shin quickstep running, and finally to 10 seconds of ankle-over-knee running action. This progression of learning can be incorporated into the warm-up.

The athlete can warm up by initially walking for 10 seconds, and then ankle-over-ankle quickstep running for 10 seconds, before doing 10 seconds of ankle-over-mid-shin running, and then transitioning into an ankle-over-knee running action for 30 seconds. This sequence should continue for 10 minutes, before resuming the dynamic warm-up.

In order to accelerate running velocity, a runner should increase the turnover rate, without shortening their stride. As noted previously, trying to run faster by lengthening the stride length not only is inefficient, it will also result in greater fatigue. Running speed can only be increased when the foot strike is moving backward faster than the center of mass is moving forward. It is important to note that too much backside mechanics occurs when the toes finish pushing off the surface, and the foot and lower leg follow-through too far behind the center of mass, resulting in a long-leg, pronounced heel strike and braking action.

As has been repeatedly pointed out in this text, considerate evidence indicates that a person's basic speed is the single most important physiological variable determining their ability to race at any distance. As such, that individual's 100m time is basic to determining that person's 400m time. Similarly, their 400m time is basic to determining their performance in the 800, 500, 3k, 5k, and 10k. Science has provided the formula for determining an athlete's potential to race in those events, computing training paces based on a percentage of the individual's 400m speed.

According to the *Track & Field Omnibook*, an athlete with greater speed can carry a given pace for a short distance with a relatively lower level of stress. This factor sets the parameters for goal-pace training. Assuming equal pace, the greater the distance of each run the greater the stress produced, even though the rest intervals are increased correspondingly. Accordingly, performing 3 x 400m at 60s, with 60s rest, produces greater stress than 30s with 30s rest. The recovery period or the time between runs, from a heart-strengthening standpoint, the work period and the rest period are both developmental. The development period can last up to 30s.

A pace that is considerably faster than race-goal pace not only achieves a developmental heart stress, it also develops a fast-twitch function in the leg muscles, a factor that is necessary for engaging in a sustained sprint at the end. The greater the number of muscle units and fast-twitch fibers recruited, the stronger the working muscles. The stronger the working muscles, the harder they can make the heart work. The stronger the heart muscle, the more oxygen-rich blood being sent to the muscles that do the work of running.

When an athlete's best potential race distance has been determined, the best way to develop race potential is by training at variable paces. Variable-pace training was conceived by British club coaches during the early 50s and 60s. During this time period, numerous world records were set using variable-pace training. The essence of the variable-pace system is to train at race-pace, plus two paces that are faster than goal-pace and two paces that are slower than race-goal pace. For example, an 800m runner would train with sprint work and 400m pace, as well as at paces at 1500 and 3k. These paces provide both speed effort and endurance. A greater percentage of work is done at race-goal pace, because the more work done at a specific pace, the more the athlete becomes efficient at running that pace.

Developing a Training Scheme

Based on the aforementioned factors, a suitable training scheme would involve four phases, as noted previously:

❏ *Phase #1: Warm-Up*

Every workout should begin with a warm-up that lasts from 15-30 minutes. Warm-ups should be dynamic in nature and involve resistance work that is specific to running and to developing the correct neurological patterns entailed in the foot strike and turnover.

❏ *Phase #2: Skill Work*

In this phase, the body is taught to work the legs, feet, and arms in a coordinated and efficient manner. While skill work can be integrated into the warm-up, it is an ongoing aspect throughout every workout.

❏ *Phase #3: Conditioning*

In this phase, the body is exposed to multitiered running velocities and exercises that are designed to concurrently enhance $v\dot{V}O_2max$, $\dot{V}O_2max$, lactate threshold, speed, speed endurance, and lactate tolerance. Learning to run systematically at perceived goal-pace is important during this session.

❏ *Phase #4: Cool-Down*

This phase entails activities that gradually bring the heart rate and body temperature back to normal. This phase can involve a variety of activities, including functional muscle strengthening. Stretching is best done during this phase, so that any spasming muscle fibers can relax and begin their recovery. Each stretch is most effective when it is held in the stretch position for approximately 60 seconds.

Each workout should last from 90-120 minutes. The warmup and cool-down phases should take up to 45 minutes during the early part of the season, and then gradually reduced as the season progresses.

CHAPTER 22

Exercises

Lower-Leg Exercises

Coaches have a number of exercises in their "toolbox" that can be utilized to develop a personalized training regimen for their athletes. This chapter details many of the more common exercises that are used by track & field coaches to train their athletes.

❏ *One-Leg Heel Raises:*

- Stand with relaxed posture, with the feet directly beneath the hips and shoulders.
- Rock forward onto the toes and hold for two seconds.
- Rock back until the heels lightly touch; simultaneously dorsiflex the ankles and flex the knees.
- Immediately, propel themselves back into tip-toe position and hold two seconds; perform 10-15 reps.

  If this exercise becomes easy, it can be repeated on the other foot.

❏ *Calf Achilles Eccentric Reach:*

- Stand about two feet back from a wall or fence, with the weight evenly balanced, and the fingertips touching either the wall or a bench for balance.
- Transfer the weight to the left foot.
- Drive the right foot up and forward as far as possible, while leaving the left foot in contact with the ground; perform 10 reps.
- Repeat this action, with the right knee turned 45 degrees to the right.
- Then repeat the action to the left.
- Next, perform the exercise with the other leg.

❏ *Max Jump and Hops With a Stick:*

- Jump straight ahead off of two feet, but land on only the right foot; then, immediately hop quickly and explosively on the right foot for five hops, while sticking the fifth landing.
- Repeat on the left foot (eight reps on each leg).

❏ *Single Leg Jumps For Distance—From Mat or Soft Surface:*

- Hop for a maximum distance on the right leg, and then hold the position for five seconds after each hop.
- Perform five reps on the right foot and then repeat on the left foot.

❏ *Platform Hops:*

- Stand behind a 6" to 11" platform.
- Lift the left foot off the ground, while flexing the left knee.
- Hop onto the platform with the right foot, and then immediately hop off the opposite side.
- Make quick contact with the ground on the right foot, and then hop forward as quickly as possible for three hops; then, begin hopping on the left foot; next, turn and hop back around the platform on the left foot over to the right; hop back onto the platform until they are in the original position and then repeat on the other foot.
- Continue for 60 seconds on each leg.

Hamstring Muscle Exercises

The hamstring muscles allow the knee and thigh to drive forward when an athlete is running. They then quickly bring the lower leg and foot back under the runner's center of mass for the foot strike. This sequential action can occur up to 100 repetitions per minute. As such, it can make the hamstring susceptible to injuries brought on by fatigue.

With regard to what factors actually cause hamstring injuries, a lack of flexibility is one of the first things that comes to mind. Some researchers, however, are convinced that hamstring injuries tend to occur more frequently, when a thorough warm-up is not used. Another theory that is advanced is that a lack of eccentric strength training is a probable cause.

The underlying basis for this line of reasoning is that the action of the hamstring muscles involves muscles that are forced to elongate, while simultaneously trying to shorten. During running, the hamstring muscles in each leg are subject to eccentric strain every time a step is taken. This can be between 90 and 100 times per minute, depending on the velocity and length of the run.

❏ *Strengthening Exercises for the Hamstrings:*

- Partners—torso falls and recovery; double leg; partner holds the feet.
- Rotated drop-offs and pick-ups with a med ball—bend forward with a med ball held at bellybutton height; rotate 45 degrees to the right; place the med ball on a bench and hold three seconds.

- Pick up a med ball and rotate back to the center and then up to the right; then perform the same action to the left; repeat six times on each leg.
- Forward lunge with a med ball—contract the glutes and hold for six seconds; perform 10 reps with each leg.
- High bench step-up with a med ball
- Foot-up squats with a med ball
- Bicycle leg swings—raise the thigh to parallel; extend the lower leg to almost fully extended and then bring the entire leg as far backward as possible.
- Partners—med ball roll—lie face down in a prone position with the legs fully extended and together; the partner rolls the ball from their butt to the ankles; contract the hamstrings and flip the ball back to the partner.
- Speed work, which helps $\dot{V}O_2$max. Speed work promotes two key physiological adaptations: a reduced rate of glycogen utilization and a smaller build-up of lactate during strenuous effort.

Total-Body Strength Exercises Through Functional Strength Activities

- Pull-ups—quick up and slow down
- Knee-up pullovers
- Bar dips—quick up and slow down
- Wheel on a bar-dip rack—15 sec. build-ups
- Feet-up push-ups
- Bench step-up
- Feet-up half-squats
- Vertical hops
- Plyo hops—triple jump
- Burpies
- Knee-up power jumps, with a sprint
- Spring running
- Standing military press
- Jerk (without the clean)

Strengthening Exercises for the Cool-down

- Crazy feet
- Plank core exercises to the front, back, and side
- Eccentric reaches—leg and knee
- Runner's pose stretch cord

Exercises to Strengthen the Kinetic Chain and Improve the Stretch Reflex Phenomenon

- Body squats
- Forward lunges
- Side lunges
- Walking lunges

- Squat hops
- Scissor hops
- V-hops (vertical)
- Bench squats
- One-leg stands (bench/pistol squats)
- Bench step-ups
- Burpies with sprint
- Power jumps with sprint
- Leg swings—hamstring and hip flexor
- Bleacher spring running
- Spring running
- Running/bounding
- Plyo jump
- Sprint up a steep incline
- Fast-relaxed running down a slight decline
- Diagonal hops
- One-leg squat with lateral hop (bench)
- Quick-forward hops
- Burpies with sprint
- Runner's pose
- One-leg heel-toe-knees and toe raises
- Tempo arm drills (15 sec buildup)
- Sprints 30-60m
- Partial one-leg squat with a jump
- Box fall with a hop
- Bicycle leg swings
- Rhythm hop
- Hip flexor leg swings

Running-Specific Exercises

- Foot-up, one-leg half-squats
- Bench step-ups
- Leg swings—hamstring and hip flexor
- Sprinting up a short, steep incline
- Running fast-relaxed down a slight decline
- 30 meter sprint with resistance
- Spring running up either a bleacher or a hill
- Quick vertical hops
- Quick forward hops for 30m
- Burpies with a 10m sprint
- Power jump with a 10m sprint
- Plyo hops—triple jump
- Box hops
- Box falls with hops
- Standing from sitting position—one leg
- Runner's pose with a stretch cord
- Single-leg heel raises
- Toe walking with opposite heel raises
- Body squats
- Walking lunges
- Squat hops
- Hamstring falls and rebound
- Wheel—running while suspended
- Lead-up lactate threshold (e.g., 50m fast, 50 easy, 100m fast, 100 easy, 150 fast, 150 easy). Perform as many as possible, and then advance to 200, 250, 300.

Exercises and Considerations to Periodize the Training Season to Compete in Endurance Races

- Strength and speed:
  - ✓ During the first third of the training season, concentrate on developing strength and power.

- Gold Medal running mechanics:
  - ✓ Learn to run fast-relaxed
  - ✓ Keep the arms and upper-body relaxed with relaxing-tempo arm movements.
  - ✓ Learn to run with a full range of movement.
- Progression of running mechanics:
  - ✓ Ankle-over-ankle
  - ✓ Ankle-over-mid-shin
  - ✓ Ankle-over-knee
  - ✓ Ankle-over-knee recovery
  - ✓ Knee-up, toe-up
  - ✓ Lower-leg extension
  - ✓ Claw-back action of foot
  - ✓ Make foot contact as far back under the center of gravity as possible.
  - ✓ Make contact with the flexible part of the foot.
- Activate as many muscle fibers as possible:
  - ✓ Emphasize fast-twitch muscle recruitment
  - ✓ 30-60m sprints
  - ✓ 50m hill charges
  - ✓ Downhill running
- Develop a quick on-and-off foot strike:
  - ✓ Quick-foot drills
  - ✓ Speed agility ladders
  - ✓ Acceleration ladder
  - ✓ Quickstep skip
  - ✓ Jump rope
- Upper body strengthening:
  - ✓ Pull-ups
  - ✓ Hanging knee-ups
  - ✓ Knee-up pull-overs
  - ✓ Bar dips
  - ✓ Military press
  - ✓ Jerk (without the clean)
  - ✓ Feet-up push-ups
- Core strengthening:
  - ✓ Plank exercise—front, back, and side
  - ✓ Med-ball rotations

- ✓ Bench dips
- ✓ Modified crunches
- ✓ Lower-back extensions
- The kinetic chain:
  - ✓ Bench step-up
  - ✓ Bench squats
  - ✓ Vertical hops
  - ✓ Runner's pose
  - ✓ Scissor hops
  - ✓ Quickstep skip
  - ✓ Power skip
  - ✓ Hamstring skip
  - ✓ Plyo box hops
  - ✓ Quick hops
  - ✓ Power jumps
  - ✓ Jump rope
  - ✓ Crazy feet
  - ✓ Hurdle hops
  - ✓ Spring running
  - ✓ Bounding

Running Workouts to Develop Strength and Power

- Running workouts to recruit the maximum number of muscle fibers:
  - ✓ Concentrate on speed and lactate conversion.
  - ✓ Speed agility and acceleration ladders
  - ✓ 30-60m sprints
  - ✓ 50m fast/50m easy/100m fast/100m easy/150m fast/150m easy
  - ✓ 100m graduated on grass, barefoot in 20m increments
  - ✓ Speed makers—50m build-up/50m all out/20m graduated down, with quick feet
  - ✓ Fartlek
  - ✓ 50m uphill sprint
  - ✓ 50m uphill spring running
  - ✓ Other work, e.g., 400- and 800-type workouts at the end of three weeks

Supplemental Exercises

❏ *Balance and Eccentric Reaches*

- Stand in a running position about 2' from a wall or fence, with the weight on the left foot.
- Reach forward with the right foot, keeping the leg straight until the toes touch the wall.
- During the reach, rotate the hips forward until the Achilles is stretched.
- Repeat 10 reps.
- Next, turn the knee to the right about 30 degrees and repeat 10 reps of reaching to the right, followed by the same movement to the left.
- Repeat these same actions by driving the knee straight ahead, while rotating the hip forward until the Achilles is on stretch.
- Repeat on the opposite leg.

❏ *Bench Step-ups*

- Stand in a running position on a bench or bleacher, with the weight on the right foot.
- Step backward with the left leg, until the flexible part of the foot touches.
- Immediately recoil the left knee forward in a runner's pose.
- As the left knee reaches forward, dorsiflex the toes and lift the center of gravity upward with the support foot.
- Repeat 10 times, and then repeat on the opposite leg.
- Progressively add more reps as strength improves.

❏ *Bicycle Leg Swings:*

- Stand with the weight balanced on the left leg.
- If necessary, hold on to a stationery object for balance.
- Drive the right thigh forward to a runner's pose, and then reach out with the lower leg.
- Immediately bring the foot backward, until the calf collapses against the hamstring.
- Repeat 10 times on each leg.
- Progressively add more reps then use a stretch cord for resistance.

Running-Specific Activities

❑ *Partial Squats:*

- Stand with the weight balanced on the left leg, with the right foot on a bench.
- Stand with the left foot far enough in front, so that the knee, when in the squat position, does not go past the support foot.
- Lower the center of gravity to a half-squat position.
- Repeat 10 reps, and then hold the 11th in the half-squat position for 10 sec.
- Take a brief break, and then repeat until three sets are completed on each leg.

❑ *Power Skip:*

- Skip on the balls of the feet, while driving each knee in to a runner's pose position.
- Then pulling the lower leg and foot back quickly under the center of mass, scraping the ground in a skipping motion.

❑ *Feet-Up, One-Leg Hops in Place:*

- Hop quickly on one foot for 30 sec then alternate - 2 sets
- Perform two sets.

❑ *Box Hop With Sticks:*

- Begin by taking quick hops on the right foot.
- Next, hop on top of the bench.
- Then quickly hop off the other side.
- Land quickly and then explode forward again, landing on the right foot.
- Take three quick hops and then land, sticking in a half-squat position.
- Repeat on each leg three times.

❑ *Hurdle Hopping:*

- Place 8" hurdles on a slight incline 3' apart, covering 20m.
- Hop up quickly on one leg three times.
- Repeat on the opposite leg three times.

❑ *Diagonal Hop:*

- Run forward easy for five steps
- Then, move diagonally to the right with the right foot.
- As the right foot strikes the ground, hop quickly in place and then explosively hop diagonally to the left, landing on the left foot.

- When the left foot strikes, hop once in place and then explode diagonally to the right.
- When the right foot hits, hop once and then explode to the left.
- Keep this rhythm for 45 seconds and then rest for 15 seconds, before resuming this rhythm for another 45 seconds.

❑ *AC-DC 100s:*

- Accelerate for 20m.
- Hold fast-relaxed for 60m.
- Gradually, decelerate for 20m. The objective is to stay as relaxed as possible during these repeat 100s.
- Complete eight 100s with an easy 30-second walk between each rep.

❑ *One-Leg Squats With Lateral Hops:*

- Assume a squat position, with the right foot on a bench.
- Then, perform a 90-degree squat.
- When the squat reaches 90 degrees, hop laterally with the left foot about 10 inches and then back to center.
- Next, hop to the right and back to center.
- Do this rhythm 2 x 12 times and then perform the same exercises on the right leg.

❑ *High Knee Explosions:*

- Stand in a relaxed running position.
- Begin by jumping three quick jumps in place.
- Then, explode with both knees, driving them upward past waist high.
- When landing on both feet, sprint 10m.
- Complete a total of 15 repetitions.

❑ *Hot Coals Running:*

- Begin by standing in a relaxed running position.
- Start running in place, using the flexible part of the feet.
- Increase the tempo of the foot strike as fast as possible during 20 seconds of quick feet.
- Imagine that you are running on hot coals.
- Keep the upper body and arms totally relaxed, moving the arms coordinated with the movement of the feet.
- After 20 seconds, relax and repeat three times.

A Training Regimen for Neuromuscular Development, Based on Running Skills, Strength, and Speed

The general strength phase should last for four weeks. During this phase of training, dynamic activities that strengthen the muscles that do the work of running are introduced. These activities are designed to increase flexibility, improve the muscle's ability to resist fatigue, and promote forceful actions and reactions.

❏ *Neuromuscular activities to implement a base for racing:*

- Learn to do dynamic warm-ups and cool-downs.
- Functional leg strength:
  - ✓ Leg swings—hamstring with a straight-leg and knee-up-toe-up bicycle action
  - ✓ Hip flexor—straight leg, with a full hip rotation
  - ✓ Bench step-up
  - ✓ Bench squats
  - ✓ Vertical hops

❏ *Activities to enhance overall body strength:*

- Pull-ups
- Bar dips
- Knee-ups
- Bent knee pull-over
- Feet-up push-up
- Bench dips
- Jerks
- Standing military press

❏ *Activities to teach foot strike and turnover, and promote Gold Medal running form:*

- Quickstep walk
- Quickstep skip
- Quickstep run, using a speed ladder
- Run-in acceleration ladder (e.g., 30m)
- Step counting—18 T.O. in 10 sec.

❏ *Running progressions:*

- Run by percentage of effort.
- Steady state runs, with alternating running velocities

- Steady state runs with Gold Medal form and step-counting
- Establish goal-training paces.
- Introduce circuit training.
- Determine the number of meters per sec./min. averaged during the run. Use proven English club coaches' formula for determining multi-tiered training paces.
  - ✓ Use five tiers of training velocities (see six-minute run test)—800 - 1600 - 3200 - 5000 -10,000.

❑ *General training guidelines:*

- Concentrate on good form for all activities.
- Begin with 10 reps for most activities.
- Systematically increase volume and intensity for the first three weeks and then back off slightly for one week.

❑ *Power and strength activities:*

- 100-meter sprint graduated uphill
- Fartlek running:
  - ✓ Increase duration of steady state runs using segments of quality.
  - ✓ Finish runs with 10 x 100m @ 3k pace.
- Plyometrics
- Multitiered velocity running:
  - ✓ 400 for speed
  - ✓ 800-1500 for speed endurance
  - ✓ 3k for running economy ($v\dot{V}O_2$max 4 - 5k for improving $\dot{V}O_2$max)
  - ✓ 10k for improving LTRV
  - ✓ 15k for general endurance
  - ✓ Increase the intensity and volume for the first three weeks and then cut back slightly during the fourth week.

❑ *Explosive strength period guidelines:*

- Increase the speed of activities, but do not sacrifice form.
- Reduce the dynamic warm-up to 15 minutes.
- Expand plyometrics.
- Increase spring running.
- Increase power running.
- Perform running bounding.
- Gradually reduce the overall volume.

- Maintain the level of intensity.
- Add real speed.
- Perform fartlek work (60 sec. @ 400; two minutes easy).
- Reduce long runs to 45 minutes.
- Do the last killer workout 10 days prior to the big race (e.g., 10 x 400 @ mile pace; 3k effort—30 sec.—30 sec.)
- Perform rhythm sets @ 120 percent $\dot{V}O_2max$ (200-300).

❑ *Specific strength activities (four-week period):*

- Introduce activities that promote balance.
- Introduce balance boards.
- Expand plyometrics.
- Expand core strength.
- Power running
- Spring running
- Bounding
- Expand the number of hill reps.

❑ *Specific strength period guidelines:*

- Increase speed when doing dynamic activities, but do not sacrifice correct form.
- Work up to 30 sec/30 sec rest.
- Increase acceleration ladders to 60m, with an emphasis on knee-up, toe-up, ankle-over-knee running action.
- Emphasize goal-pace training (e.g., 30 sec. to 3 min./30 sec. @ $\dot{V}O_2max$/300 to 500 @ 800/300 to 600 @ mile pace/600 to 1000 @ 3k/800 to 1200 @ 5k./1200 to 3000 @ 10k:
  ✓ Long runs (e.g., 60-70 min/30 min/45 min/60 min/70 min)
  ✓ Use segments of quality during run.
- Perform as many activities while running barefoot as possible.
- End the workout with some kind of speed work.
- End every workout with stretching.

❑ *Tapering:*

- During the last two weeks, reduce the volume of training by 30 percent.
- Rest two days prior to the biggest race.
- Do easy 20 min., followed by 400m rhythm reps x 3; concentrate on running rhythm and relaxation.

REFERENCES

Anderson, O. Best training methods to improve aerobic capacity. *Running Research News*, Vol. 2 (6), pp. 1-2, 5-6, 1986.

Anderson, O. Extra miles and workouts don't help novice marathoners. *Running Research News*, Vol. 11 (2), pp. 1, 5-6, 1995.

Anderson, O. Let your mind control your heart—and make you a better runner. *Running Research News*, Vol. 12 (10), pp. 1-4, Dec. 1996.

Anderson, O. Mental strategies for runners. *Running Research News*, Vol. 1 (2), Sept.-Oct. 1985.

Anderson, O. Running economy remains elusive to even the most earnest experts. *Running Research News*, Vol. 5 (5), pp. 1, 3-5, Sept.-Oct. 1989.

Anderson, O. Things were so easy until $v\dot{V}O_2max$ and then $tlimv\dot{V}O_2max$ had to come along. *Running Research News*, Vol. 15 (2), pp. 1-5, 1999.

Anderson, O. Things your mother forgot to tell you about cross training. *Running Research News*, Vol. 11 (6), pp. 1, 5-7, 1995.

Anderson, O. Torrid new $v\dot{V}O_2max$ sessions keep you at $\dot{V}O_2max$ and are easier to carry out. *Running Research News*, Vol. 16 (7), pp. 1-4, 2000.

Billat, V. et al. The concept of maximal lactate steady state: A bridge between biochemistry, physiology, and sport science. *Sports Medicine*, Vol. 33 (6), pp. 407-426, 2003.

Bowerman, W.J. and Freeman, W.H. *Bill Bowerman's High-Performance Training for Track and Field* (3rd ed). Monterey, CA: Coaches Choice, 2009.

Burgomaster, K. et al. Effect of short-term sprint interval training on human skeletal muscle carbohydrate metabolism during exercise and time-trial performance. *Journal of Applied Physiology*, Vol. 100, pp. 2041-2047, 2006.

Carr, G.A. *Fundamentals of Track and Field* (2nd ed). Champaign, IL: Human Kinetics, 1999.

Cavanagh, P.R and Williams, K.R. The effect of stride length variation on oxygen uptake during distance running. *Medicine & Science in Sports & Exercise*, Vol. 14 (1), pp. 30-35, 1982.

Daniels, J. and Daniels, N. Running economy of elite male and elite female runners. *Medicine & Science in Sports & Exercise*, Vol. 24 (4), pp. 483-489, 1992.

Dellinger, B. and Freeman, B. *The Competitive Runner's Training Book* (2nd ed). Monterey, CA: Coaches Choice, 2018.

Ecker, T. *Basic Track & Field Biomechanics* (4th ed). Monterey, CA: Coaches Choice, 2015.

Fatigue and exercise part 1A: The pacing strategy—why the "obvious" is crucially important. Retrieved Dec. 21, 2008 from www.sportsscientists.com/2008/05/fatigue-and-exercise-part-i.htmlhttp://www.sportsscientists.com/2008/05/fatigue-and-exercise-part-i.html.

Hamilton, R. et al. Effect of high-intensity resistance training on performance of competitive distance runners. *International Journal of Sports Physiological Performance*, Vol. 1 (1), pp. 40-49, 2006.

Heinert, L.D. et al. Effect of stride length variation on oxygen uptake during level and positive grade treadmill running. *Research Quarterly for Exercise and Sport* (RQES), Vol. 59 (2), pp. 127-130, 1988.

Karp, J.R. 101 *Developmental Concepts & Workouts for Cross Country Runners*. Monterey, CA: Coaches Choice, 2010.

Kyrolainen, H., Avela, J. and Komi, P.V. Changes in muscle activity with increasing running speed. *Journal of Sports Science*, Vol. 23 (10), pp. 1101, 2005.

Kyrolainen, H., Belli, A. and Komi, P. Biomechanical factors affecting running economy [Abstract]. *Medicine & Science in Sports & Exercise*, 2001. Retrieved Feb. 10, 2017 from http://www.ncbi.nlm.nih.gov/entrez/query.fcgi?db=pubmed&cmd=Retrieve&dopt=citation&list_uids=11474335&query_hl=4&itool=pubmed_docsum.

Lafortune, M., Valiant, G. and McLean, B. Biomechanics of running. In: Hawley, J. (Ed.). *Running* (pp. 28-43). London: Blackwell Science Ltd., 2000.

Leedy, M.G. Commitment to distance running: Coping mechanism or addiction? *Journal of Sport Behavior*, Vol. 23 (3), 2000.

Lyden, R.M. *Distance Running*. Ashland, OR: The Running Book, LLC, 2003.

Markovic, G. and Mikulic, P. Neuro-musculoskeletal and performance adaptations to lower-extremity plyometric training. *Sports Medicine*, Vol. 40 (10), pp. 859-895, 2010.

Mikkola, J. et al. Concurrent endurance and explosive type strength training improves neuromuscular and anaerobic characteristics in young distance runners. *International Journal of Sports Medicine*, Vol. 28 (7), pp. 602-611, 2007.

Morgan, D.W. and Martin, P.E. Effects of stride length alteration on racewalking economy. *Canadian Journal of Applied Sport Science*, Vol. 11 (4), pp. 211-217, 1986.

Morgan, D.W. et al. Factors affecting running economy. *Sports Medicine*, Vol. 7 (5), pp. 310-330, 1989.

Niemi, A.K. et al. Mitochondrial DNA and ACTN3 genotypes in Finnish elite endurance and sprint athletes. *European Journal of Human Genetics*, Vol. 13, pp. 965-969, 2005.

Noakes, T. et al. Peak treadmill running velocity during the $\dot{V}O_2max$ test predicts running performance. *Journal of Sports Sciences*, Vol. 8 (1), pp 35-45, 1990.

Paavolainen, L. et al. Explosive strength training improves 5-km running time by improving running economy and muscle power. *Journal of Applied Physiology*, Vol. 86 (5), pp. 1527-1533, 1999.

Paavolainen, I., Nummela, A., Rusko, H. and Hakkinen, K. Neuromuscular characteristics and fatigue during 10km running. *International Journal of Sports Medicine*, Vol. 20, pp. 516-521, 1999.

Rukso, H. and Bosco, C. Metabolic response of endurance athletes to training with added load. *European Journal of Applied Physiology and Occupational Physiology*, Vol. 56 (4), pp. 412-418, 1987.

Slawinski, J.S. and Billat, V.L. Difference in mechanical and energy cost between highly, well, and non-trained runners. *Medicine & Science in Sports & Exercise*, Vol. 36, pp. 1440-1446, 2004.

Steadman, M. *Coaches' Guide to Cross Country and Track and Field Training Cycles*. Monterey, CA: Coaches Choice, 2015.

Taskin, H. Effect of circuit training on spring agility and anaerobic endurance. *Journal of Strength & Conditioning Research*, Vol. 23 (6), pp. 1803-1810, 2009.

Telaneus, S. and Jordan, S. *Developing a Successful Cross Country Program*. Monterey, CA: Coaches Choice, 2005.

USATF. *Track & Field Coaching Essentials*. Champaign, IL: Human Kinetics, 2014.

USATF. *USA Track & Field Coaching Manual*. Champaign, IL: Human Kinetics, 1999.

Williams, K.R. Biomechanics of running. *Exercise and Sports Science Reviews*, Vol. 13, pp. 389-441, 1985.

Williams, K.R. and Cavanagh, P.R. Relationship between distance running mechanics, running economy, and performance. *Journal of Applied Physiology*, Vol. 63 (3), pp. 1236-1245, Sept. 1987.

ABOUT THE AUTHOR ━━━━━━

The first nine years of my life, which were spent in eastern Oklahoma, were hard times during the 1920s and 30s. Dirt farming was the way of life. We had no money and by today's standards, we would be at considered poverty level. We survived by the barter system, as there was very little cash to be had. I can honestly say that I was born in a real log cabin that my grandfather built, when he homesteaded a plot of land in the Cherokee Nation. Only my mother's sister was in attendance at my birth, and it was three days later that the doctor came to see me. As an infant, I survived pneumonia, whooping cough, measles, chicken pox, mumps, and an intestinal disorder that were all treated with castor oil, except for my malaria, which was treated with doses of quinine. We did not know we were poor, because everyone else was living the same existence. Like hundreds of thousands of others, we were able to make our way to California in 1936, where we were immediately informed and constantly reminded that we were "white trash." Fortunately, there was work harvesting the various crops.

Although my parents had only an eighth-grade education, they made sure that my brother and I went to school every day. They impressed upon us the value of reading, writing, and arithmetic. I was eager to learn and liked to express myself, which lead to being president of our eighth grade class, and, subsequently, president of our senior class. I loved sports and activities that involved running. I learned to run barefoot, since we had to save our only pair of shoes for winter. During recess in grammar school, I would tease the older boys so they would chase me around the schoolyard satisfying my need to run. I left high school in the middle of my senior year in 1944 to join the Navy, given that I had no desire to be drafted into the Army.

While in the Navy, I became close friends with another "Okie" whose dad was a track coach at Oklahoma State. It was through this relationship that I decided to pursue a career in physical education and coaching. In September 1946, I enrolled at Wayne State University in Detroit, Michigan, which is another story. I tried out for the basketball team but was cut after the first week.

I then found the cross-country coach, who immediately issued me a pair of Chuck Taylor canvas running shoes. I competed for two seasons in cross-country and one season in track, running the mile and two mile. I was very fortunate to have Dr. David L. Holmes as my coach and mentor. It was from him that I learned my coaching skills and adopted his philosophy of training. I did not like the weather in Detroit, and put myself on a fast track for graduation. Dr. Holmes offered me the opportunity to be a student assistant coach for 65 cents an hour, plus mileage.

The highlight of my coaching time at Wayne State was taking our sprinters to the 1948 Penn Relays. These four talented athletes won the 4 x 100, 4 x 200, long jump, and placed second in the 100 meter. One of the athletes, Lorenzo Wright, went to the

1948 Olympics in London, where he placed 4th in the long jump and ran a leg on the 4 x 100 relay that won. The team, however, was disqualified and later declared the winner after a review of movie film of the race.

My first coaching and teaching job was at Maxwell High School, a small farming town in the northern Sacramento Valley, where I coached all sports and taught five periods of classes during my four-year tenure. Subsequently, I worked at Fillmore, Fort Jones, and Buena High Schools—all in California, covering a 17-year period. During my 17 years of coaching at the high school level, I learned to coach all events, which prepared me for my 22 years of coaching all events at Humboldt State University in Arcata, California.

The environment at Humboldt State was ideal for endurance athletes. A year-round mild temperature, with a variety of terrain in an inspiring setting at a college that offered outdoor science programs attracted many endurance athletes to the program. My first national champion was Gary Tuttle in the steeplechase. I had coached Gary at Buena High and followed him to Humboldt State a year later. Our philosophy of training at HSU was to run as many miles as possible as fast as possible, without sustaining a debilitating injury. The terrain and weather made it possible to develop that theory to the fullest, which resulted in 11 national champions and 64 All-Americans between 1966 and 1988. I also trained Mark Conover in the marathon, who won the 1988 Olympic Trials Marathon. While at HSU, he was a 5- and 10- kilometer national champion.

During my last 10 years at HSU, I became acutely aware of the importance of proper running mechanics and its role in running economy and overall racing performance. In 1985, Dr. Owen Anderson started publishing his *Running Research News*, which presented scientific research articles authored by noted scientists in the field of physiology of exercise. Information in these articles altered many of my theories of training athletes to compete in endurance races.

During the past 20 years, I have formulated a training scheme that combines the neuromuscular aspects of running with the development of the cardiovascular system. I firmly believe that all of the physiological variables of endurance exercise should be developed concurrently, as opposed to one before another. My training scheme philosophy is at odds with the traditional long distance training theory that demands that a season begin by first developing an aerobic base through a buildup of mileage before adding the development of other physiological variables.

I have applied my theory of training at two-year (Sierra Junior College) and four-year (UC Davis) colleges, as well as at the youth, high school, and master levels, with a considerable amount of success. I believe coaches must teach proper running mechanics, functional leg strength, and the neuromuscular aspects of running, concurrently with enhancing speed endurance and aerobic power, in order to develop the complete runner.

Jim Hunt was inducted into the U.S. Track & Field and Cross Country Coaches Association Hall of Fame in 2013.

A Time for Reflection

As I look back at my childhood, I see a young boy running barefoot over grass, dirt, and rocks in a creek bed. I remember running for the sheer joy of running. Today, as I observe three- and four-year-olds at play, I see them having fun and seemingly running every place they seek to go. I see them relaxed and totally uninhibited with short, quick steps and coordinated arm movements, a natural phenomenon of exercise.

At the end of 63 years of coaching, I have made a complete circuit, high school, junior college, four-year college, international, and back to high school. When I observe 14- and 15-year-old runners now in the first days of track or cross-country workouts, I ask myself, what happened to those three- and four-year-olds who are now high school runners who want to give competitive running a try? When I see them now, they seem to have acquired inhibitions and run with a style that seems lumbering, and definitely not natural or relaxed.

I can only guess that at the age of three and four, most children have very few restraints in their daily lives and their movements reflect this situation in their running. I suspect that somewhere around the fourth or maybe fifth grade, the pressure of rules and restraints placed in their daily lives combined to build a negative effect on their psychological makeup. These inhibitions profess themselves in the form of restricted and unnatural movements in their running. Poor running posture, straining, and slow foot and arm action typifies the beginning runner at the entry level of high school track and cross-country. Coaches have a difficult task teaching these young athletes to be able to relax their upper body and arms, as well as, how to place the foot strike so that excessive energy is not wasted during the act of running. When you think about it, beginning runners, those individuals with some previous training, as well as those who are well-trained, all have the same needs when it comes to improving their potential to race in endurance events. At the beginning of the season of training to race, all athletes can follow the same basic training scheme and develop to their potential level of fitness. It is just a matter of making adjustments within the scheme to fit the fitness level of each athlete.